PROJECT BASED LEARNING
MADE SIMPLE

PROJECT BASED LEARNING
MADE SIMPLE

BY APRIL SMITH

CLASSROOM-READY ACTIVITIES THAT INSPIRE CURIOSITY,
PROBLEM SOLVING AND SELF-GUIDED DISCOVERY
FOR THIRD, FOURTH AND FIFTH GRADE STUDENTS

Ulysses Press

Published in the United States by:
Ulysses Press
P.O. Box 3440
Berkeley, CA 94703
www.ulyssespress.com

ISBN: 978-1-61243-796-5
Library of Congress Control Number: 2018930762

Printed in Canada by Marquis Book Printing
10 9 8 7 6 5 4 3 2 1

Acquisitions editor: Bridget Thoreson
Managing editor: Claire Chun
Editor: Shayna Keyles
Proofreader: Renee Rutledge
Front cover/interior design and layout: what!design @ whatweb.com
Cover artwork: © elenabsl/shutterstock.com

Distributed by Publishers Group West

This book is dedicated to my two amazingly curious kids, who I hope will experience classrooms with project-based learning when they enter school.

TABLE OF CONTENTS

CHAPTER 4
MATH AND FINANCIAL LITERACY **83**

INTRODUCTION

If you're reading this book, you've either done project-based learning (PBL) before and are looking for new project ideas, or the concept is totally new to you. Either way, I'm ecstatic that you want to bring quality project-based lessons to your classroom.

I discovered project-based learning a few years into my teaching career. I had recently moved to a Title I school, and it was very apparent that regular teaching methods were not going to cut it with my students. The traditional teaching structure I had been using at the time was teach, practice, assess, repeat. There was no real-life application of the standards.

As I was trying to figure out what to do with my class, I thought back to when I was in school. I wasn't the ideal student. I was easily bored, and I preferred to do my own thing. If a lesson didn't hold meaning for me personally, I disengaged. But I had one teacher in particular that had no trouble engaging me in her lessons. Almost everything she taught was rooted in real-life application, and there was always a hands-on component. All of this was on my mind when our instructional coach introduced us to something the district wanted to start seeing in our classrooms quarterly: project-based learning. I jumped in feet-first.

I'd love to tell you that it was an instant transformation, but it wasn't. It was very messy at first. I had to learn how to effectively plan the lessons, incorporate the standards, and manage my classroom during the activities. But now, it's an integral part of my classroom.

It's my sincere hope that this book helps make project-based learning easy for you and your students. The activities are organized by focus subject because this is the organizational structure that most teachers feel most comfortable with. However, you will find that skills from other subject areas will naturally connect with every topic. Remember that project-based learning is best when it incorporates multiple subject areas and is customized to your individual classroom. I'll teach you how to customize these projects in Chapter 2, where I offer suggestions for making connections in every project idea.

CHAPTER 1

PROJECT-BASED LEARNING BASICS

Project-based learning is a teaching method where students gain and apply skills by working on a long-term project that involves an in-depth inquiry into a topic or question. It can be used to teach students completely new skills and practice skills they already have a basic understanding of.

Knowing the basic elements of project-based learning is an important part of using PBL in your classroom. Teachers that struggle to find success with PBL are often missing one of these key elements. If you find yourself having difficulty, return to these elements, or check Common Issues on page 256.

ELEMENTS OF PROJECT-BASED LEARNING

Significant content. The project should be focused on curriculum-based knowledge and skills that relate to grade-level standards. This is why choosing a topic is so important.

21st-century competencies. Project-based learning includes skills that are valuable for today's world, such as problem solving, critical thinking, collaboration, communication, and creativity. Most students do not naturally know how to collaborate and communicate effectively, so these skills often need to be explicitly taught within the structure of a project.

In-depth inquiry. The biggest piece of your project will be inquiry into a topic. The process of in-depth inquiry includes asking questions, researching, and discussion.

Driving question (DQ). This guiding question focuses the entire project. It should be open-ended and pique student interest.

Need to know. In order to show students why they need to learn about certain concepts and skills, you need to frame your project within a realistic scenario. I have my students keep a record of what they need to learn using a "Need to Know List" during each of my projects.

Voice and choice. The key to engagement in project-based learning is allowing students to make their own choices. This doesn't mean that students should do whatever they want, but with teacher guidance and scaffolding, they should choose their end products and decide how they work.

Critique and revision. Critique is meant to help students get feedback in order to improve upon their products. Always build several critique opportunities into your PBL, and have your students get into the habit of writing down specific questions they want answered about their work. After they receive feedback, they will need to make revisions based on the feedback.

Public audience. In most cases, a public audience should be people outside the classroom or school that students can present their end products to. When you choose an audience for your PBL, remember that the best audience is always one that's meaningful and appropriate for the project. Sometimes this is an outside audience, and other times it's an audience inside your building. Each project idea included in this book suggests an audience that fits with that topic.

This might seem like a lot to plan for just "one" lesson, but it's important to remember that a project-based learning activity can last for several weeks and hit many skills and standards that span multiple subject areas. Compared to other types of teaching, I've found that I do far less tedious planning when implementing PBL.

CHAPTER 2

CUSTOMIZATION AND PLANNING

When I train teachers and administrators on the project-based learning planning process, I provide them with two simple forms: a brainstorming page with the elements of PBL, and a pacing calendar that includes a general plan of daily goals. I've found that the daily lesson plan really varies from teacher to teacher, so I don't include a form for that. My advice to you is to do your daily lesson planning in whatever format works best for you. The brainstorming page and pacing calendar will make it easy to write your daily lesson plans.

CUSTOMIZING PROJECT IDEAS

It's impossible to write one lesson plan that works for every single classroom. Additionally, standards vary greatly from state to state, and country to country. This is why I've left the project ideas in this book pretty general, overall. I want you to mold the project-based learning activities within to fit your students and your own personal style.

The project ideas in this book can be easily modified to cover different topics or standards. Let's look at an example of how you can customize one of the projects to make it more relevant for your classroom.

ORIGINAL PROJECT IDEA

ANIMAL HABITATS

Spotlight on: Habitats

Driving question: How can we plan a suitable habitat for the zoo's newest animal addition?

Audience: Zookeeper or biologist

PROCESS:

1. Begin this project by visiting your local zoo, or taking a virtual field trip to one. During the field trip, have students take notes on the different habitats they see.

2. After the field trip, lead a discussion on some of the elements of the habitats for a few key animals. Compare and contrast what they observed about these different animal habitats.

3. Discuss why it's so important to have a habitat suitable for each of the specific animals. This would be a great time to have your students read more about the habitat of one of the animals they saw during their field trip. You can check out books from the library about a variety of animals and their habitats for the class to share, as well as assign students to research individually.

4. Bring in guest speakers that are experts on this topic, like a biologist or zookeeper. Contact your local zoo or conservation area ahead of time. If you can't find someone locally, try to connect your class with an expert via video chat.

5. When your students have a good grasp on what a habitat is and why it's important, introduce your driving question. Have students work in small groups to choose an animal they would like to see the zoo add to their animal exhibits.

6. Have students conduct in-depth inquiry into what will be necessary in order to build a suitable habitat for their chosen animals.

7. Student end products should include a written plan, habitat design, and any other media that will convince the zoo to choose their idea. Their end products should show that they have a good understanding of the climate, food, and sensory needs of the animal.

Other Connections: Include STEM concepts by having students build working models of their animal habitat.

Let's say that your community does not have a zoo, but your school is located just a few minutes from the Monterey Bay Aquarium. You still want to teach your students about animal habitats, but you know that talking about the zoo won't have the same relevance as working with the local aquarium where you and your students can visit and interact with habitats up close.

MODIFIED PROJECT IDEA

AQUARIUM HABITATS

Spotlight on: Habitats

Driving question: How can we plan a suitable habitat for the aquarium's newest addition?

PROCESS:

1. Start off this project by visiting the Monterey Bay Aquarium.

2. After the field trip, lead a discussion on some of the different habitats that the students observed. Which marine organisms shared a habitat? Do they think this was done on purpose?

3. Discuss the planning process behind each aquarium habitat. Bring in a presenter from the aquarium to explain why it's so important to have a habitat suitable for a specific organism. This would be a great time to have your students read more about the different animals they observed on their field trip.

4. When your students have a good grasp on the different habitats inside of the specific tanks and exhibits in the aquarium, introduce your driving question. Have students work in small groups to choose an animal they would like to see the aquarium add to its animal exhibits.

5. Have students conduct in-depth inquiry into what will be necessary to build a suitable habitat for their chosen animals. Have students research the other marine organisms that can share the habitat with this animal.

6. Student end products should include a written plan, habitat design, and any other media that will convince the aquarium to choose their idea. Their end products should show that they have a good understanding of the needs of all of the organisms that will be occupying that habitat.

Other Connections: Include STEM concepts by having students build a working model of the animal habitat.

Smaller modifications can be made, as well. It's expected that you will sometimes need to tweak the driving question and audience to better suit your classroom.

For example, you can update the driving question "How can we keep our community safe from severe weather hazards?" to reflect the specific grouping in your classroom.

A small change can make the structure more specific: How can my group help keep our community safe from severe weather hazards?

DIFFERENTIATION

When I first heard about project-based learning, I was hesitant to try it because I had many students labeled special education or ELL (English-language learner). I thought that PBL was just for the "higher level" kids, and that it would be a nightmare to differentiate for each student. I'm glad that I didn't let this misconception stop me from trying project-based learning.

You already know that one of the essential elements of project-based learning is student choice and voice. Not only do students have a choice in how to show what they've learned in the product they create, but they also have several choices throughout each project. For example, in the aquarium habitats project, students are able to choose the animal and all pieces of their habitat. They're also able to choose additional media to use in their presentations. These choices allow students to determine not only where they want to go with their project, but also how to get there. Everyone works to answer the same driving question, but the answer can be found with whichever strategies and tools work for the individual student. PBL gives students a chance to learn through technology, text, art, multimedia, and much more. It accommodates every learning style and ability level.

What I've learned through doing project-based learning with a variety of students is that PBL has a lot of natural differentiation built in. I don't need to plan differentiation in the way I used to, but I do still keep a few things in mind when planning my projects.

Individualized education program (IEP). I review all IEPs before beginning a project to make sure that I make any necessary modifications to meet the individual needs of these students. If I think there are additional tools that will help them, such as calculators or reading selections from a different reading level, I make sure to have those available.

Grouping. I try to mix students that have different skills so that each student is an active learner in their group. For example, if I have six students that have shown they are gifted artists, I split them into separate groups so that each of them is the artistic "expert" in their group. I do the same with my problem solvers, leaders, bookworms, and creative thinkers. This way, students learn the content through the medium they are strong in. My artists learn about habitats by designing the elements of one, while my bookworms learn through reading every book they can on the topic.

Rubrics. Rubrics are a fair way to grade students on their individual contributions to the project. Just one rubric allows you to grade every student at their individual level, based on their individual contributions. Student-friendly rubrics also tell students your expectations for the project and help you justify the grades you've given them. See more about rubrics on page 252.

Enrichment. Sometimes we forget to differentiate for our advanced learners. Keep a list of tasks or questions for these students that push them past the level other students are learning at. It's always a good idea to look at the related standards in the next few grade levels to get ideas to use with advanced students.

Encourage these students to think outside the box and come up with innovative ideas for the project.

TECHNOLOGY

The good news is, there isn't a specific amount of technology you need in order to run a successful project-based learning activity. I've successfully done PBL with varying levels of technology.

STUDENT 1:1 DEVICES

Incorporating laptops, tablets, and other devices should be explicitly planned into the project-based learning activity. Decide how these devices will be used every step of the way. Are there certain apps that would augment the experience? If they will be using the internet to search for information, which sites will they use, and how will this research be done?

Decide which digital tools your students will use to take notes throughout the project. You will need to have an organizational strategy so that every student is consistent with the organization of materials. Brainstorm ways that you can help students be efficient with managing their time on these devices. One way I like to help my students stay on track is to prepare a folder of related images before we start the project. This way, students don't get bogged down scrolling through thousands of pictures in search.

If you are having students search the internet during their research, I recommend using Sweet Search (www.sweetsearch.com), or another student-friendly search engine.

SOME STUDENT DEVICES

Some are better than none, right? When we did project-based learning and only had a few student devices available, I had to be very strategic with how we used them, because we couldn't do activities that required everyone to use a device at the same time. I used the devices mainly as support stations for students to look up tough questions or find something special for their end products.

For researching, we use a variety of kid-friendly magazines and books. I cleared our public and school libraries out of every book on the PBL topic. I played videos and did virtual field trips with the whole group. I printed piles of pictures that we kept organized in small tubs. I also tried to get as many guest speakers as possible to come speak to our class.

NO STUDENT DEVICES

I've been in this situation, as well. If you have no student devices, your teacher computer will be your main hub for all of your tech needs. Use my advice above regarding research materials, and try to incorporate technology in ways that only require one computer. A really popular way to incorporate technology into project-based learning is to have guest speakers talk to your class over the video-chat platform Skype. This will allow your students to learn from an expert that isn't local, or doesn't have the time to visit in person. You can also use this platform to collaborate with students in other classrooms, which is a great way to augment the PBL experience!

PLANNING

Planning is key to the success of your project-based learning activities. Over the years, I've simplified my planning into two steps: brainstorming how I will incorporate each element of PBL, and creating a calendar to show a rough pacing of the activity. I do the first step in a simple table or spreadsheet.

PLANNING AN ENTRY EVENT

An entry event is essentially the project kickoff. This is what you do to get students engaged in the PBL activity right off the bat. Many of the project ideas in this book have suggestions for a basic introduction activity, but there are many ways to kick off your project.

Here are some ideas I have used in the past to get my students hooked on the premise of a project-based learning activity:

- Dress up to match your theme: Come into your classroom dressed up to match your theme or to depict the project's target audience. This is a great way to show students that they're going to be doing something really important in class.

- Read a fun story: Find a picture book that tells a story that's relevant to your project. Read it to your students, and discuss why the author wrote a story on this topic. You can then lead straight into asking the driving question and researching some of the elements of the topic.

- Show an interesting video: YouTube is a great resource for all kinds of videos. If your topic lends itself to a short, exciting video, then show one to kick off the PBL. If you plan on doing a virtual field trip, show your students a teaser video about the place you will be visiting virtually.

- Make a picture slideshow: Find some interesting photos that go well with your topic, and begin the project with a slideshow of these images. Have students discuss what they notice about the images. Use this to model discussion procedures during PBL time.

- Bring in a guest speaker: Bringing in an expert is a great way to make the project more meaningful. Have them come in ready to speak on the topic, and maybe even demonstrate something related that will capture the students' attention.

- Introduce your audience: Make a profile of your audience for your students. In a couple of my project ideas, your students will be making a product for kids five and under. You might bring in some of these kids to help introduce the topic and audience.

BRAINSTORMING: ELEMENTS OF MY PROJECT-BASED LEARNING ACTIVITY

This table gives you prompts to use when brainstorming. I recommend creating a spreadsheet or table with the elements of PBL, similar to the brainstorming guide below, that you can fill in when you begin planning a new project-based learning activity. You can return to this page as a guide each time you fill in your brainstorming table.

The example that follows shows what my brainstorming would look like if I were beginning the planning process for the Aquarium Habitats project.

BRAINSTORMING GUIDE: ELEMENTS OF PBL

SIGNIFICANT CONTENT	Include specific details about the topic your students will explore. Add standards and skills that relate to this topic.
21ST-CENTURY COMPETENCIES	Tell which competencies you will build into this project, and how you plan to explicitly teach students these skills.
IN-DEPTH INQUIRY	How will your students learn about this topic? What resources will be available to them for researching their questions about the topic?
DRIVING QUESTION	What will your driving question be? Mold the DQ that is included with the project to your own classroom.
NEED TO KNOW	What skills or content will your students need to know to successfully complete this project? How will they learn this information?
VOICE AND CHOICE	What choices will students have during this project?
CRITIQUE AND REVISION	List the opportunities you will give students for critique and revision. I recommend building at least a quick feedback session into each day.
PUBLIC AUDIENCE	Who will your students present their final products to? Take the suggested audience from the project and mold it to fit your classroom.

BRAINSTORMING EXAMPLE: AQUARIUM HABITATS

SIGNIFICANT CONTENT	Students will: Explore habitats for different marine life using in-depth research and discussion. Learn how being a part of a group helps animals obtain food, defend themselves, and cope with changes (LS2.D) by discussing what they observed at the aquarium. Write an opinion piece that explains what their plan is and why it should be chosen for the next aquarium habitat. Standards: Habitats NGSS 3-LS4-3, NGSS LS2.D, CCSS.ELA-LITERACY.W.3.1
21ST-CENTURY COMPETENCIES	Critical thinking: I will model for students how to research problems and choose the best possible solution. Collaboration: I will have my groups set "group norms." I will have each student create a list of skills they have that relate to the project, so that group jobs and responsibilities can be easily assigned. Groups of four will be assigned. Communication: I will facilitate discussions that help students grow their communication skills. I will mix up the discussions so that they get practice communicating with different peers, guest speakers, and me.
IN-DEPTH INQUIRY	Students will explore habitats using a variety of resources. Source 1: Monterey Bay Aquarium's Habitat Webpage Source 2: *Water Habitats* by Molly Aloian and Bobbie Kalman Source 3: PBS Learning Media: Habitat: Animal Homes (az.pbs learningmedia.org/resource/nat15.sci.lisci.anihome/habitat-animal-homes) Source 4: Image and video folder created to share with students
DRIVING QUESTION	How can we plan a suitable habitat for the aquarium's newest addition?

NEED TO KNOW	Students will need to understand what a habitat is and why it's important. This will be learned through scaffolded research and discussion. They need to know how to organize and write a logical plan for their aquarium habitat proposal. I will model how I write my own plan, as well as provide students with a lot of opportunities to get feedback from their peers and adults. They also need to know how to write an opinion essay, so I will sprinkle in mini-lessons on opinion writing.
VOICE AND CHOICE	Student groups will initially choose the animal they want to build the aquarium's new habitat around. They will work collaboratively to make research-supported choices for the habitat, including the other marine organisms that will share this habitat. They will make all design choices.
CRITIQUE AND REVISION	Students will be encouraged to seek out feedback from their peers and adults when they have a question about their plan. They will connect with other groups for a quick, 5-minute feedback session at the end of every period. During these sessions, the group will bring two or three questions that they want the critiquing group to answer about their work. A longer critique session will take place at the end of every large task the students create. During one of these sessions, they will get feedback from two of the aquarium's marine biologists. This will be done remotely on Skype.
PUBLIC AUDIENCE	Aquarium Director

PACING

One of the most common misconceptions about project-based learning is that it is 100 percent student controlled. There's a big difference between students controlling the project and student-led inquiry. I have seen many teachers fail and give up on project-based learning because there was no structure in place for their students.

Both kids and adults thrive in structured environments that allow latitude for individual choice and input. Too much structure, and we lose buy-in. Too little structure, and we lose focus. It's a balancing act, and it takes practice to get it right. The good news is, properly scaffolded project-based learning will give your students the exact amount of structure they need to become self-directed learners.

The most common complaint I hear from teachers about project-based learning is that their students don't know how to properly use their project time. This is why I always recommend that teachers have a list of general tasks that will allow the project to progress at a sufficient pace. This is where the pacing calendar comes in. Your pacing calendar provides a general plan of what targets or goals you want your students to meet each day. The majority of the PBL time will be left open for scaffolded student-led inquiry, but even that time block should have a clear purpose each day.

PACING CALENDAR

	INTRODUCTION / MINI-LESSON	STUDENT PORTION	WRAP-UP
DAY 1 STANDARDS/ SKILLS: NGSS 3-LS4-3	Aquarium Director speaks about the process of adding a new habitat to the aquarium.	Students set group norms. Have them research and discuss animal habitats. They should make preliminary choices on what animal they'd like to see in a new habitat.	Share animal ideas with the Aquarium Director so that she can give students feedback.
DAY 2 STANDARDS/ SKILLS: NGSS 3-LS4-3	Work as a class to create an organization scheme for recording the information they learn about their chosen animal's habitat.	Gather and discuss information on this animal's habitat using a variety of resources.	Check in: Are students confident in their animal choice? Do they have proper information on the habitat?
DAY 3 STANDARDS/ SKILLS: NGSS 3-LS4-3	Create a task list as a class that addresses the steps of creating a plan for this new habitat. Make sure that all "Need to Knows" are incorporated in the list.	Students begin completing the tasks on the task list. Continue asking questions and conducting research that enriches the students' plans for the habitat.	Review task list. Find out where students are on the task list.

DAY 4 STANDARDS/ SKILLS: NGSS 3-LS4-3	Model how to cite sources to support student ideas. Group discussion: What does every habitat need (food, shelter, and protection)?	Return to groups to plan, taking into account what new ideas they learned from the discussion.	Review task list. Find out where students are on the task list. Introduce tomorrow's main focus.
DAY 5 STANDARDS/ SKILLS: NGSS LS2.D	Share a few YouTube videos on marine symbiotic relationships.	Students should have a good list of what to include in their habitats. Guide students into their research on other animals that will complement this habitat.	Critique and revise: Share ideas for animals that will share the habitat. Get feedback and revise (either adding or removing animals from this list).
DAYS 6–7 STANDARDS/ SKILLS: NGSS LS2.D, 3-LS4-3	Discuss design options. Look at digital drawing tools and available supplies for non-digital designs.	Students begin designs of habitat. Continue researching each component. Students should know exactly what each part of their aquarium is and where it should go. They should be supporting these choices with evidence from several sources.	Peer critique and revision of habitat plans.
DAYS 8–10 STANDARDS/ SKILLS: NGSS LS2.D, 3-LS4-3	Complete group critique (Day 8). Days 9–10, revisit task lists and set end product goals.	Main revision: Finalize habitat plan design. Work on end products/presentations. Schedule presentations with the Aquarium Director.	Go over presentation time and format.

DAYS 11–14 STANDARDS/ SKILLS: CCSS W.3.1	Give mini-lessons on the writing process (opinion writing).	Students turn written plans into opinion essays. Follow the writing process and incorporate writer's workshop.	Prepare written plan, habitat design, and any other media into a digital or print portfolio. Present on the date set with the Aquarium Director. Grade using rubric.

TASK LISTS

In the example above, students drive the project by coming up with a class task list. This solves a problem that many teachers have when starting project-based learning: Their students lack independence and struggle to decide what to do next. I pace the project out with my guess as to what they will include on their task lists, but my pacing calendar is flexible and is often changed from day to day. It's important to scaffold the creation of a task list. Your students should be a part of the discussion, but you want to make sure you are helping them organize this list. Here's an example task list for the Aquarium project:

- Research the physical items our animal needs in their habitat.
- Draw our first habitat design.
- Research what food our animal needs. Design a feeding area for our habitat.
- Revise our habitat design.
- Finish our habitat designs.
- Complete our written plan.
- Put together our final presentation.

As I stated earlier, the purpose of pacing the project out is to keep the project moving along a manageable timeline. Without pacing and task lists, projects can be completed too quickly, and students miss out on in-depth inquiry. On the flip side, the teacher and students can lose focus and it can become a never-ending project.

SUPPLIES

There isn't a set list of supplies you'll need for project-based learning. I suggest making a list of materials you'll need when planning an individual project. Send a letter to parents letting them know all about the project before you begin. Warn them that their students may request supplies, depending on what they are creating for their projects. This letter is also a good opportunity to ask for parent volunteers if you want assistance during the project.

CHAPTER 3

SCIENCE AND STEM

1 ANIMAL HABITATS

What kid doesn't love the zoo? Teach your students about animal habitats by actually having them research and create a suitable habitat for the zoo. Virtual field trips, guest experts, and hands-on learning make this activity a hit!

Spotlight on: Habitats

Driving question: How can we plan a suitable habitat for the zoo's newest animal addition?

Audience: Zookeeper or biologist

PROCESS

1. Begin this project by visiting your local zoo, or taking a virtual field trip to one. During the field trip, have students take notes on the different habitats they see.

2. After the field trip, lead a discussion on some of the elements of the habitats for a few key animals. Compare and contrast what they observed about these different animal habitats.

3. Discuss why it's so important to have a habitat suitable for each of the specific animals. This would be a great time to have your students read more about the habitat of one of the animals they saw during their field trip. You can check out books from the library about a variety of animals and their habitats for the class to share, as well as assign students to research individually.

4. Bring in guest speakers that are experts on this topic, like a biologist or zookeeper. Contact your local zoo or conservation area ahead of time. If you can't find someone locally, try to connect your class with an expert via video chat.

5. When your students have a good grasp on what a habitat is and why it's important, introduce your driving question. Have students work in small groups to choose an animal they would like to see the zoo add to their animal exhibits.

6. Have students conduct in-depth inquiry into what will be necessary in order to build a suitable habitat for their chosen animals.

7. Student end products should include a written plan, habitat design, and any other media that will convince the zoo to choose their idea. Their end products should show that they have a good understanding of the climate, food, and sensory needs of the animal.

Other Connections: Include STEM concepts by having students build working models of their animal habitat.

2 SAVE THE BEES!

There has been a huge decline in the bee population, but your class can help! Your students will learn about the plight of the bees and come up with innovative ideas to help the local bee population. This real-life science project is a great way to make a difference in your community.

Spotlight on: Adaptation

Driving question: How can we come up with an innovative idea to help the local bee population?

Audience: Local beekeeper or gardener

PROCESS

1. Introduce the topic by reading articles about the declining bee population. Have students use a graphic organizer to record reasons why the population is in decline.

2. Find out more about the local bee population by interviewing a local plant expert or beekeeper, or asking them to come speak to the class. Make sure that your students are familiar with the type of bees found in your community, and what their purpose is.

3. Compile data about the decline in the local bee population. If you can't find this data, modify this project by choosing a region that has seen a more alarming decline in population.

4. Have students work in small teams to come up with different ideas to help increase the local bee population. Have each individual student journal about their ideas.

5. Have each group submit a proposal with their solution. Proposals should describe any materials or plans for anything they need to build or buy.

6. Choose one or more ideas to implement as a class. Have families and other community members come in to help pull it off. Seek donations from local businesses if you need any supplies. Big home improvement stores are usually happy to help!

7. Have your students complete their journals with a reflection on the project. In a few months, return to the journal to reflect on how the project has made a difference to the local bee population and environment.

Other Connections: Write an opinion essay about why the idea(s) your class chose should be used in other areas of the country to help the bee population.

3 WEATHER-RELATED HAZARDS

Every region has specific severe weather events that its inhabitants need to be prepared for. Help your students understand the importance of being informed about natural hazards while helping the community prepare.

Spotlight on: Weather and natural hazards

Driving question: How can we keep our community safe from severe weather hazards?

Audience: Local community

PROCESS

1. Introduce this topic by showing a video of a recent severe weather event. Discuss how people in the affected region prepared for that event.

2. Research types of severe weather using picture books, passages from your science book, and videos.

3. Explore the National Weather Service's Storm Prediction Center website (spc.noaa.gov). Discuss the types of severe weather that are noticeably prevalent in each region. Then, look specifically at the region you live in.

4. Have students inquire into local severe weather hazards. Provide news articles from past fires, floods, tornadoes, or storms. Have students make a list of severe weather events that have happened in the area in the last 20 years.

5. Further inquire into the hazards that this severe weather creates. Begin discussing how your class can prepare the community for these hazards in the future. Start a list of ways you can help the local community prepare. Possible ideas are making emergency kits, creating brochures with steps on what to do in case of a severe weather emergency, and creating a video PSA (public service announcement).

6. Decide as a class which one thing you want to do to help the community prepare. Contact community leaders with expertise in your topic so you can get help completing and distributing the end product. For example, if your students want to make a video PSA about severe weather, a local TV station and the mayor or someone on the city council would be a great help in making your project a reality.

7. Make a list of what tasks need to be done to complete this product.

8. Create smaller groups within your class to handle different tasks. Bring in family and community members to help. Contact local businesses if you need certain supplies or services donated.

9. Schedule a time to present this project to the community.

Other Connections: Standards related to maps and graphs fit in well with this project. The Storm Prediction Center (spc.noaa.gov) has color-coded maps for tornadoes, fires, and storms that your students can get information from.

4 CLIMATE CHANGE

Climate change is a problem that your students will deal with for most of their lifetimes. Get your students thinking about the impact while helping a plant or animal that is already suffering from the effects of climate change.

Spotlight on: Environmental hazards

Driving question: How can we help a plant or animal whose environment is changing due to climate change?

Audience: Climate scientist or biologist

PROCESS

1. Have students create a KWL chart[1] about climate change to see what they already know about the topic. Inquire about climate change using different types of reading material, images, and videos. The NASA Climate (climate.nasa.gov) and Climate Kids (climatekids.nasa.gov) websites provide a wealth of information on the topic.

2. Have students create a list of the effects of climate change. Under each effect that students put on their list, have them brainstorm a list of the plants and animals they think are being affected by that effect. Make a list of these animals as a class.

3. Do a little research into the list your students create to make sure that you can find information online about how the animals they chose have been affected by climate change. Finalize your list, then have students choose which animal from the list they are most interested in helping.

---

1 A KWL chart has three columns labeled "What We Know," "What We Wonder," and "What We Learned."

4. Create groups based on student choice. I suggest having students choose a plant or animal before telling them you will be putting them into groups, so that they choose based on their interests and not on friend groups.

5. Contact local scientists, or biologists in the areas where these animals live. Set up a way for your students to video chat or email these experts with questions.

6. In their groups, have students further inquire into the plight of their plants or animals.

7. Have groups write down ideas for how they can help their plants or animals overcome the effects of climate change.

8. Have each group choose a final idea and create a proposal. If their idea involves something they can create a model or demonstration of, have them do so.

9. Have students submit their proposals and videos of their model or demonstration to the experts for feedback. This can all be done using live chat or through email.

10. Choose one plant or animal. As a class, implement the ideas to help this plant or animal.

11. Have students reflect on the impact of their projects.

Other Connections: You can raise money to help a plant or animal, which will allow you to easily incorporate math standards.

5 THE NIGHT SKY

Every night, young children look up at the twinkling stars in the night sky. Your students will help teach these children about what they're looking at, all while learning more about the topic themselves. This project has students creating something for a young audience, so they will have to be able to explain about constellations in a simple, easy-to-understand way.

Spotlight on: Earth and the solar system

Driving question: How can we recreate the constellations for young children?

Audience: Young children

PROCESS

1. Decide which audience you want your students to create their constellation projects for. It may be kindergartners in your school, a local preschool, or younger siblings of the students in your class. You can visit these kids through live video or in person when it is time to share the final products.

2. Introduce the topic by showing students a picture of the Big Dipper and having them work together to form this constellation with their bodies.

3. Provide students with photos of different constellations. This can be done by sharing links as a part of a WebQuest, printed photos, or library books.

4. Have students begin their inquiry by making a list of questions about the topic. Questions will sound like "What are the constellations made up of?" and "How do the stars make those shapes?"

5. Have students research their questions. They should discuss and write notes when they find the answers to their questions. If they have additional questions as they research, they should write those down, too.

6. Tell students that they are going to recreate the constellations for young children. This can be done in any way they'd like to do it. They may want to create a book, models, or something more innovative. I suggest grouping students in pairs for this project.

7. Decide as a class what type of product will be created. Work together to recreate the constellations for your audience. Have students include important information about the constellations that they learned in their research.

8. Present the product when it's ready.

9. Have students each write a three- to- five-paragraph essay to reflect on their end product and explain what they learned about constellations.

Other Connections: Connect art to this lesson using the painting *The Starry Night* by Vincent van Gogh.

6 JOURNEY AROUND OUR SOLAR SYSTEM

Most universities have a space science program, and they're very accommodating to young students interested in that field of study. Connect with local college professors and their students to work on a path for a future space probe.

Spotlight on: Earth and the solar system

Driving question: How can we plan a path for a space probe to study our solar system?

Audience: Professors or students in a space science program

PROCESS

1. Introduce the topic by showing students any educational video about NASA space probes from the past, present, or future. NASA has a wide variety of these videos on their YouTube channel.

2. Help students investigate the orbits of the Earth, sun, and moon.

3. Expand the investigation to all the planets in our solar system. Have students draw a model of the solar system, showing each planet's relationship to the sun.

4. Have students find other photos and videos of NASA space probes so that they can familiarize themselves with what probes look like and what equipment they carry. You can share specific pages and videos from the NASA website that have information on this topic.

5. Through discussion, have students decide what parts of the galaxy they want their probe to explore. Are there specific planets they want to explore? Do they want to focus on learning more about supernovas?

6. Facilitate while students work in small groups to discuss the possible routes of a space probe. Have them draw it out or make models. Once they have a route that they can support, have them research the distance between each of the probe's destinations (planet, moon, or sun). They should add this information to their drawings or models.

7. If the college professors you reached out to were willing, have them ask their students to provide feedback to your class. This can be done remotely over Skype or email.

8. Have students brainstorm creative ways they can present the probe's path to their audience. They will work in their small groups to create these presentations.

9. Work with the college professors to assign a specific audience to each group. You may be able to have each group present directly to a professor, or it may work out better to have them present to groups of college students. This depends on what works best for all teachers involved. Make sure that your students' audience gives them final feedback and uses a rubric to assess their final products.

Other Connections: Make a math connection by having students calculate the total distance that the probe will travel on its journey.

7 BRING THE SOLAR SYSTEM TO LIFE

A lot of planning and research goes into museum exhibits. In this activity, students will use the same research process to create an interactive solar system exhibit.

Spotlight on: Earth and the solar system

Driving question: How can we create an interactive exhibit of the solar system for a science exhibit?

Audience: Kids of all ages

PROCESS

1. Before beginning, determine where students will set up the exhibit. It would be fantastic to have the exhibit in a place that all kids in the community can gain access to, but some place in your school would work, as well. If you're interested in making this a community outreach project, contact your city leaders or any local organizations that cater to children.

2. Take a virtual or in-person tour of a science museum that has interactive exhibits geared toward children. Have students take notes of what is included in the exhibits and what appeals to them personally.

3. Tell students that they will be creating their own interactive exhibit that displays the solar system for kids their age.

4. Have students research what types of things museums around the country display in their space exhibits. Tell them to write down what they observe in the exhibits they see on museum websites and then research information about each topic. For example, if they see an exhibit that models the orbits of the planets in our solar system, they can research everything there is to know about these orbits and make their own models on paper.

5. Brainstorm ideas for the exhibit as a class. Continue to research as you discuss ideas as a class.

6. Decide as a class what you want to include in the exhibit. Come up with five or six different parts of the exhibit.

7. Split students into small groups to design and discuss different parts of the exhibit. Create these groups based on each student's individual interest. Encourage students to continue researching the topic as they design their piece of the exhibit.

8. Put design ideas onto paper or large posters. If you have devices, use them for the design. After students have received critique and revised their piece several times, bring all pieces of the exhibit together into one design.

9. Gather the materials needed for the exhibit. Begin planning as a class for how you will put the pieces of the exhibit together.

10. Build the exhibit using your class plan. While building, create online and print materials to tell people about the exhibit before and during their visit.

11. Put on the exhibit. Allows students to act as docents and share what they learned with kids visiting the exhibit.

Other Connections: Incorporate business and math skills into this project by discussing the financial side of the museum you visited on your virtual tour. Talk about how the museum makes money and what costs they incur when creating a new exhibit.

8 SCHOOL GARDEN

A school garden is the perfect way to observe nature! This project is a great way to make connections with the community while creating something wonderful for your school.

> **Spotlight on:** Plant structures
>
> **Driving question:** How can we build a school garden to help the students at our school learn about nature?
>
> **Audience:** School leadership, staff, and students

PROCESS

1. Before beginning, create relationships with anyone that can help teach your students about gardens. If you live near a college with an agricultural program, they may be willing to send students to help teach about and build the garden. There may also be school staff members or parents that have knowledge to share.

2. Secure funding for the garden. There are many grant opportunities available for school gardens. Local and chain home improvement stores will often donate supplies. You can even add a fundraising element to this project, having your students raise the money and gather necessary supplies.

3. Introduce the topic by showing photos and videos of various school gardens. If a school nearby you already has a garden, see if you can set up a visit to see it in person.

4. Introduce the elements necessary to create a school garden. Use this opportunity to discuss plant functions and what the garden needs to thrive.

5. Research and choose different plants for the garden. Have students record the requirements for maintaining these plants, including the climate they grow best in. Use this information to narrow down the plants that will grow best in your school's garden.

6. Work together to find a good location for the garden, keeping plant functions in mind.

7. Have students work in groups to create virtual gardens that map out what the garden will look like. There are many free online garden design tools that your students can use for this step.

8. Put together the best elements from each group's design to make the final plan for the garden.

9. Build the garden. Your class can also work together to create pamphlets for the other students that will visit the garden. These pamphlets can inform about how to take care of the garden and teach about plant structures.

Other Connections: After students understand plant structures, use this understanding to teach them about animal structures.

9 URBAN GARDEN

Hydroponics is very relevant to today's world. Indoor hydroponic systems are being called "urban gardens" because they are prevalent in urban areas where it's difficult to find the land for a large outdoor garden. Help your students learn the basics of hydroponics by having them create their own urban gardens.

Spotlight on: Plant structures

Driving question: How can we learn to grow food inside to feed our families and community?

Audience: Community members with interest in urban gardening

PROCESS

1. As with the School Garden activity on page 47, make connections with some people in the community that have experience with hydroponics. If you live near a college with a hydroponic lab, they may be willing to send students to help teach about and build the garden. There may also be school staff members or parents that have knowledge to share.

2. Bring in speakers and show students pictures of creative urban gardens. There are some amazing photos online of the innovative ways people have created hydroponic systems in their homes!

3. Research what hydroponics is and the benefits of a hydroponic system. Discuss why the name "urban garden" is used to refer to some types of hydroponic systems.

4. Research and make a list of what is needed for hydroponics. Examine each type of hydroponic system and work together as a class to determine which will work best for your needs.

5. Compare and contrast the difference between a traditional garden and a hydroponic system.

6. Make a list of fruits, vegetables, and herbs that students are interested in growing. Narrow down the list to a few plants.

7. Have students split off into groups. Assign each group a plant.

8. Work together to design what your classroom's hydroponic system will look like. Make a list of materials needed.

9. Bring in volunteers to help set up the hydroponic system.

10. Plant your seeds. Work with your students to maintain the system and observe what happens as the seeds grow.

Other Connections: Discuss other ways we solve problems in food using science, such as the use of GMOs.

10 ENERGY CONSERVATION

You'll be a hero to your administration when you implement this project! Your students will create a guide of ways that the school can conserve power, saving energy and money. This guide can also be distributed to other schools in your district.

Spotlight on: Energy

Driving question: How can we find ways for our school to conserve energy, in order to save money and help the environment?

Audience: School leadership, staff, and students

PROCESS

1. Teach students about energy transfer and related energy standards. Use videos, hands-on activities, and other opportunities for in-depth inquiry.

2. Discuss the reasons for conserving energy.

3. Have students share ways they conserve energy at home. Have them discuss the topic at home and bring in any additional ideas they learned from these conversations.

4. Make a copy of the school map. Tell students that you will be touring the school looking for ways to conserve energy. Discuss areas to focus on, like vents, air filters, thermostats, doors, windows, and lights. They should be thinking about fixes and substitutions that will conserve energy in each area.

5. Start with an evaluation of your classroom. Have students work in pairs, writing down notes on the map of ways to conserve energy. Model asking questions like, "Is this room too warm or too cold?" and "Is there anything using energy that we aren't using?"

6. Repeat Step 5 in other areas of the school. By the end of your tour, students should have notes jotted down for several areas, including the office, cafeteria, and library.

7. Share ideas and have students work in pairs to make a list of the ways energy can be conserved in each room. Have them research the cost of replacing or fixing any items. Bring in someone from your maintenance staff to discuss the costs of things like replacing weather stripping. Some things will be free, like moving items that are blocking vents and changing the thermostat a few degrees.

8. Have each pair create energy conservation guides for your school. These guides should include suggestions for conserving energy in each area of the school, and ways for other teachers to conserve energy in their classrooms based on the inefficiencies you found in your own classroom.

9. Include a cost list in each guide. Have students add up the total cost of implementing all their ideas. Costs will vary on each guide since students will be making their own individual recommendations.

10. Have students prepare the guides to be distributed to people in the school and around the district. Let them decide how they want to present the guides.

Other Connections: Have students write opinion essays on the importance of energy conservation. This project also has a clear connection to mathematical standards, when students calculate the costs of their suggestions.

11 EARTHQUAKE!

Students love studying earthquakes. In this project, your students will work in small groups to build seismographs to record a simulated the earthquake. This project incorporates both engineering design and study of natural hazards.

Spotlight on: Natural hazards

Driving question: How can we use technology to lessen the impact of earthquakes on people?

Audience: Seismologists

PROCESS

1. Before beginning, make a connection with a local university or group of seismologists. If you can't make a connection locally, contact the National Weather Service or a university that has a specialized seismology program. See if you can get a presenter, or someone willing to give feedback on your projects.

2. Begin by discussing how earthquakes are caused and the effects of earthquakes.

3. Hand students a blank map of North America. Pull up the USGS Earthquake Hazards Program website (https://earthquake .usgs.gov/earthquakes/map) and have students record the recent earthquakes shown on their map.

4. Use YouTube to find appropriate videos of earthquakes to share with your students. Focus on videos where the magnitude is stated. You want students to observe the difference in values on the magnitude scale.

5. Have students conduct research to find out how earthquakes are measured. Once they determine that seismographs are used to measure earthquakes, tell them to research how seismographs work and build their own. Have them work on this in small groups. Give students access to everyday materials they may need, such as wire, string, paper, pencils, markers, pens, paper clips, poster board, cardboard, foil, rubber bands, tape, trays, etc. They can also bring items from home that they think will help with their design.

6. After students have built and tested their seismographs using a simulated earthquake in the classroom (for example, shaking a desk that it's placed on), have them evaluate the effectiveness of their designs and the designs of the other groups. Students can continue to revise their designs until they are satisfied.

7. Have students discuss how using this technology can positively impact human life. One likely answer is that seismographs allow us to warn people of the possibility of a tsunami after an earthquake. Have them brainstorm ways that the seismograph can be improved upon to have an even larger impact.

8. Have groups take photos or video of their seismographs to send to the seismologist or other connection you made. Ask that person to give a little feedback to the class. They can also discuss the future of this instrument and how it is being improved upon.

9. Wrap up the project by having students share their seismographs with other classrooms, explaining their purpose and how they work.

Other Connections: Discuss the engineering design process while students build their seismographs.

12 IT'S ALIVE!

One of my favorite ways to teach students about insects is to have them create their own insect! During this project, students will have to learn a lot about insects in order to create one that is superior to all others.

Spotlight on: Insect structures

Driving question: How can we use knowledge of insect structures to create our own insects?

Audience: Students at other schools

PROCESS

1. Have students research the three regions of an insect's body. Have them draw and label these regions on different types of insects.

2. Tell students that they will be designing their own insects, either by putting together parts from different insects or coming up with their own. Encourage them to think about what insects can do, and try to design a superior insect.

3. Have them discuss and brainstorm ideas for their own insect. They will need to have a plan for how they want the head, thorax, and abdomen to look.

4. Allow students to continue researching different types of insects to familiarize themselves with the different "designs" of each region. Have them observe what they notice about each insect and continue to discuss, ask questions, and research.

5. When they're ready, have them begin designing their insects.

6. Have them get feedback and revise their designs. Make sure that they can explain the purpose for the designs of each region.

Ask them what their designs allow the insects to do. Does the insect fly? What kind of vision does it have?

7. Have students finalize their designs. Make sure that they label each region. Have them each write a short essay explaining the purpose of their overall design and what each feature allows the insects to do.

8. Have them share with other students. I suggest having students upload their images to a collaborative website so that people can see all their different designs, or finding a different public sharing space. Come up with a plan to share this. Students can share individually with friends and family members that go to other schools. You can also create a relationship with a teacher at another school to share the designs.

Other Connections: Teach students how to write descriptive paragraphs when they are explaining their insect's design. Students can also write opinion pieces explaining why their insects are superior to regular insects.

13 BUTTERFLY GARDEN

A butterfly garden is a great way to spruce up your campus. This project will help you establish a beautiful butterfly garden that can be observed by students for years to come!

Spotlight on: Ecosystems

Driving question: How can we create a butterfly garden to help beautify our campus?

Audience: School leadership, staff, and students

PROCESS

1. Show students photos of butterfly gardens. Discuss the benefits of a butterfly garden, including ecosystem and habitat conservation.

2. Have students do research to find out which butterflies are common in your area. Tell them to note places in your community where they see butterflies.

3. Have students research the types of plants that attract butterflies and grow well in your region. Explore the importance of "host plants" and "nectar plants."

4. Students should work together to decide which plants they want to use in the butterfly garden.

5. Visit the area of the school where you will plant your butterfly garden. Have students work in pairs to draw plans for the garden. Remember to keep the driving question in mind. The garden needs to be aesthetically pleasing.

6. Review student plans and work as a class to incorporate the best ideas into a final plan for the garden.

7. Have students each write a proposal for the garden, using the final garden plan as a guide. This proposal should include information on the benefits of the butterfly garden, where it will be planted, and how it will be used by students in your school. Include a copy of the final garden plan and a list of materials needed for the project.

8. Submit some of these proposals to local businesses that you think may be willing to help with the project.

9. Gather all materials and get help planting the garden. Follow your plan closely.

10. Once the garden is established, have students observe the butterflies. They can learn about the butterfly life cycle and keep records of changes in types and numbers of butterflies. Use the garden to learn about how an ecosystem works.

Other Connections: Use writing and design skills to create a butterfly field guide for the people that visit your butterfly garden.

14 THE ROCK CYCLE

This fun hands-on activity is a great way to have your students teach other students about the rock cycle. Find a location and schedule a time to showcase your awesome geology exhibition.

Spotlight on: Rocks and minerals

Driving question: How can we create an exhibition for young geologists?

Audience: Younger students

PROCESS

1. Split students into small groups to create exhibits for your rock cycle exhibition. Have students research and record information on the rock cycle.

2. Use the information students gathered to brainstorm ways to exhibit the rock cycle. Show students photos of science exhibits at local museums. Discuss what a special exhibit is and how putting one on at school can help teach other students about science. Remind students to continue to look at photos and videos of the rock cycle as they come up with innovative ways to teach about it in their exhibits.

3. Have each group submit a proposal for their exhibit. The proposal should include a sketch of the exhibit and an explanation of what it will include. Encourage students to go beyond posters. You want them to incorporate sound, video, and interactive elements.

4. Have students make any materials needed for the exhibit. These could include promotional posters, letters explaining the project to parents, and guides to give to students that attend. Provide multiple opportunities for feedback while they create their exhibits. Your students should continually improve upon their ideas.

5. Finalize exhibits and display them all in one place. Invite other students to visit the "exhibit hall" to learn more about the rock cycle.

Other Connections: As students build their exhibits, discuss the engineering design process.

15 TRAVEL THE WORLD: BIOMES

Travel planning is an important skill that incorporates many subject areas. In this fun travel project, focus on traveling the world to visit each of the world's major biomes: aquatic, desert, forest, grassland, and tundra.

Spotlight on: Biomes

Driving question: How can we make family travel plans to visit each of the world's major biomes?

Audience: Families

PROCESS

1. Define the word biome.

2. Make a list of biomes and have students collect images of each. They can find these images online, or you can bring in books on different biomes for students to use during their inquiry.

3. Print a map of world biomes for each student. Tell students that they are going to plan their own trip around the world to visit each of the world's major biomes.

4. Have students ask questions about each biome, then research the answers. As they begin to understand each biome, they can research where these biomes are found in the world.

5. Each student will need to pick a place to visit for each biome. For example, to visit a tundra, options include northern Alaska, Canada, Norway, Finland, Sweden, or Russia. Have students mark each place they will visit on their maps.

6. Help students prepare their travel plans by researching airports and travel options. Their final plan should show their flight paths to get to each location, beginning at your closest airport.

7. For students that want to make more in-depth trip plans, have them research how they will get from each airport to a specific place or sight they want to visit.

8. Have students put their travel plans together and present them to their families.

Other Connections: Have students research the number of miles they will fly from one place to the next. Integrate math skills using mileage and trip costs.

16 MATTERCHEF

In this delicious project-based learning activity, your students will learn about matter as a part of a class cooking show. This activity does involve using burners, so I suggest having parent volunteers to help with safety.

Spotlight on: Matter

Driving question: How can we create a cooking show that displays different states of matter?

Audience: Kids with an interest in cooking

PROCESS

1. Have students research matter. Focus on solids, liquids, and gases. Watch videos so students can observe what each state of matter looks like.

2. Show students examples of cooking shows. You can find quite a few that feature young chefs on YouTube. Tell students that they will be working in small groups, and each group will be creating a small cooking demonstration for your class cooking show. Use the driving question to remind students that the focus of this cooking show will be on different states of matter.

3. Have groups come up with ideas on how to demonstrate the states of matter in cooking. To show the transition from solid to liquid, they will most likely want to melt something. For this, you will need an electric griddle or a burner and pot. These can easily work with any plug in the classroom, but you will need extra supervision when students are using them.

4. Have students discuss their ideas and get feedback. They should continue researching matter and revising their cooking demonstrations until they're ready.

5. Meet with each group individually to approve their demonstration idea and make a materials list. Discuss the language they will use in their demonstration when they explain how they are displaying the forms of matter.

6. Film the demonstrations. You can do this one group at a time or all at once, if you have the capability to do so.

7. Combine all the demonstrations into one video. Have students help you edit the demonstrations, adding in subtitles and sound effects.

8. Share the cooking show. You can upload it to YouTube, your class site, or your school's social media channel.

Other Connections: Use measuring tools while cooking to familiarize students with units of measurement.

17 SPECIAL DELIVERY

In this special project, students will have a very good reason to learn about forces and motion: to create a proposal for a private space company. They'll discover that what they learn in school has real-life application.

Spotlight on: Forces and motion

Driving question: How can we design the next rocket for a private space company to use to carry supplies to the International Space Station (ISS)?

Audience: Private space companies

PROCESS

1. Introduce the topic by showing students videos of rocket launches to the ISS. Have them observe what they notice about the rockets.

2. Introduce each of Newton's Laws of Motion. Have students discuss each law and see if they can apply them to what happens in a rocket. For example, once a rocket is in motion, it won't stop until a force is applied.

3. Have students research the different private companies involved in the space industry. Discuss the differences between public and private space travel.

4. Show students the different components of the rockets that currently take supplies to the ISS. Discuss how these companies get the payload where it needs to go, using what they need to know about forces and motion. SpaceX has information on their website about the Falcon 9, including design elements and cost. The biggest chunk of their in-depth inquiry should be done during this step.

5. Have students create a design for the next rocket to visit the ISS. Have them label the necessary components of the rocket. Tell them to decide which private company they are designing the rocket for, and to include the company's logo in the design. They can design their rockets on paper or on their devices.

6. Display final products. Share online and even send designs to the companies that students chose to design rockets for.

Other Connections: Have students write a descriptive essay about their rockets. Display the writing pieces with their designs.

18 SPREAD OF DISEASE

Sometimes the best lessons are the gross ones! During this project, students will learn about the spread of disease before creating a plan to help prevent the spread of disease at your school.

Spotlight on: Viruses and bacteria

Driving question: How can we prevent the spread of disease at our school?

Audience: School leadership, staff, and students

PROCESS

1. Make a list of websites with information on the spread of disease for your students to use when conducting research. These websites should teach students about viruses, bacteria, and microbes. CDC.gov and PKIDS.org are two great resources.

2. Begin with a discussion on how germs spread. This should be prior knowledge for most students this age. Talk about hand-washing techniques and how they prevent the spread of disease.

3. Have students split off into groups, asking each group to focus on one way that viruses and bacteria spread:

- Through the air
- Hands to food
- Hands to other people
- Droplets (from sneezing or coughing) to other people
- Food (raw meat) to hands to other food

4. Have each group create a poster demonstrating the method of disease spread that they were assigned.

5. After sharing and hanging the posters around the room, have students create a KWL chart about disease spread. Make a list of important vocabulary words, including viruses, bacteria, and microbes. You can also include any specific types of viruses or bacteria that you want students to learn more about.

6. Have students write questions about their "Want to Knows" from their KWL chart and vocabulary list.

7. Have students research their questions using the materials you gathered in Step 1. Have them discuss and record answers in small groups.

8. While researching, form three larger groups. Assign a topic to each group: hand washing, vaccines, and food preparation.

9. Have each group work together to tackle these issues within your school. They can do this by creating a campaign educating students about these issues, for example.

10. After research is finished and they have tackled their assigned topic, have students reflect on the results. Revisit the project in 30 days to see if what the groups did is still helping your school.

Other Connections: Have students use informational writing skills to create handouts and other literature on the topic.

19 OUR CLASS AQUARIUM

In this project, your students will really learn how the aquarium ecosystem works when they help you set up and maintain a classroom aquarium. If you don't have room in your classroom, or already have a thriving aquarium, this project can be done in the school office.

Spotlight on: Ecosystems and interdependence

Driving question: How can we create an aquarium ecosystem in which the inhabitants thrive?

Audience: Students and visitors

PROCESS

1. Begin by showing students a video of an aquarium. Many aquariums have live feeds of their tanks that you can view on their website.

2. Have students make a list of the living and nonliving things they observe in the aquarium.

3. Next, set students up to research each of the items they observed at the aquarium. They need to find out why these living and nonliving things are in the tank.

4. Through discussion and research, have students determine what the creatures and things in the aquarium depend on to survive. Create a web that shows both dependent and interdependent relationships. A few relationships are shown in the beginning web below. Have students continue to add to their web and make relationship connections, researching until their web is complete.

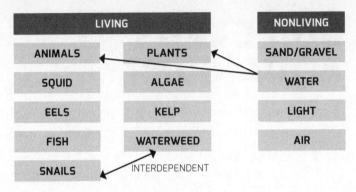

LIVING		NONLIVING
ANIMALS	PLANTS	SAND/GRAVEL
SQUID	ALGAE	WATER
EELS	KELP	LIGHT
FISH	WATERWEED	AIR
SNAILS	INTERDEPENDENT	

5. Discuss interdependent and dependent relationships.

6. Determine what size aquarium will work best for your space. Share ideas for what you want to put in your small aquarium.

7. Separate students into groups to research different aspects of the aquarium. Create a class list of supplies needed and a relationship web like the one you made for the aquarium you observed. If you will be using school funds or getting donations, submit your list of supplies as soon as it's complete.

8. Come together daily to put your research together and work as an entire class to fill in your relationship web and make concrete plans for the aquarium.

9. When all aspects have been researched, purchase all the supplies for the aquarium and set it up. Plan for how it will be maintained and assign different weeks to different groups of students.

Other Connections: Connect to math standards by estimating the cost of the supplies needed for the aquarium.

20 MARS COLONY

The idea of living on Mars is a very intriguing concept. This project is a great way to make the topic of ecosystems relevant to today's work in science.

Spotlight on: Ecosystems

Driving question: How can we create a human ecosystem model for the first colony on Mars?

Audience: Environmental biologist or biology student

PROCESS

1. Make a connection with a local environmental biologist, university professor, or biology student that knows a lot about ecosystems. Work out times for them to talk to your students about ecosystems and give them feedback on the ecosystem models they will create.

2. Invite your expert to talk to your students about what ecosystems are and what resources and social systems make up the human ecosystem.

3. Discuss what an ecosystem looks like in your local community. Then, have students make drawings of what they think the human ecosystem looks like on Earth. Students should make a list of resources that humans need to survive.

4. Discuss what an ecosystem might look like on Mars. Have students research Mars to find out how it differs from Earth in terms of resources. Make a list of challenges that humans might face on Mars.

5. Have students begin working independently on their first sketches of what a human ecosystem might look like on Mars.

6. Organize students into small groups or pairs. Have them discuss the ideas in their sketches and research the plausibility of each idea. Continue research until each group/pair has a final draft of their Mars ecosystem.

7. Have students get feedback from your expert before creating models. Facilitate their final revisions.

8. Have students use household materials to create 3D models of their human ecosystems on Mars.

9. Submit their final ideas to your expert. You can also take pictures and video to share their ideas online.

Other Connections: Habitats are an important part of an ecosystem. You can easily incorporate habitats, sustainability, and biomes into this topic.

21 CLASS PET

Even everyday life in the classroom is an opportunity for project-based learning. Include your students in choosing your classroom pet. They will learn a lot of important skills in the process!

Spotlight on: Animal habitats

Driving question: How can we select the best classroom pet and create a proper habitat for them within our classroom?

Audience: Teacher

PROCESS

1. Teach about what a habitat is. Explore examples of habitats for a variety of animals.

2. As a class, make a list of class pet ideas. Research each pet's habitat and other needs. Narrow down the list to around five plausible class pets.

3. Have students vote on their top two class pets from the list, then graph the data.

4. Determine which pet is the best fit for your class, using the data to guide you. Most often, your students will end up going with the pet that was chosen by the most students. However, they need to keep in mind the cost of the pet and teacher preferences.

5. Once your students have chosen a pet, have them split into groups to create a habitat proposal. Have students continue to research this pet's habitat in depth and come up with ideas on how to adapt it to the classroom environment.

6. Come together as a class and make final decisions about the pet's habitat, using the best elements of each group's proposal.

7. If necessary, figure out how to raise money and get supplies for the pet.

8. Set up the pet's habitat in the classroom before the pet arrives. Create a plan for how the pet will be taken care of on a daily basis.

9. Welcome your new classroom pet!

Other Connections: Have students practice their informational writing skills by creating brochures about how to take care of the pet they chose. These brochures will be helpful for classroom guests and families the pet visits during school breaks.

22 KEEPING TODDLERS SAFE

This is an extremely fun project-based learning activity that your students and their families can all relate to! You will hear a lot of giggles during this activity, especially when students test their products.

> **Spotlight on:** Magnets
>
> **Driving question:** How can we use magnets to keep a baby or toddler from opening a door or cabinet?
>
> **Audience:** Parents of toddlers

PROCESS

1. Before beginning, order many magnets in different sizes and shapes. You can also ask parents to send in baby-proofing products that are no longer needed or didn't work properly. Take a look around your classroom and school for areas where your students can test their products when it comes time. Do you have low cabinets or light doors that toddlers can easily open?

2. Recruit a parent to come in and talk to your class about their problem: None of the baby-proofing products they've bought can seem to keep their toddler out of doors or cabinets. I'm sure you won't have any trouble finding a parent with this problem.

3. Have students experiment with magnets. Encourage them to write down questions they have about how magnets work.

4. Have students research their questions and experiment with different sizes and shapes of magnets. Incorporate all information that students need to know about magnets to meet your local science standards.

5. Once your students understand how magnets work, have each student begin to design a mechanism that uses magnets to keep a door or cabinet closed. Have them draw their initial ideas on paper or design on a device.

6. Split students off into small groups. Have each group work together to test ideas using magnets and any other household supplies they can find. They will need to test ideas, do more research, refine their designs, and then test again.

7. Once each group has landed on a final design, have them test it. Have parents bring in their toddlers to help test designs. This is the most fun part of the project!

8. After this "field testing," students may have to make revisions.

9. Once they are ready to finalize their product, have each group work together to design packaging, instructions on using, and marketing materials. Students can create commercials or other types of advertisements to explain the benefits of their product.

10. Have students show the revised products to families.

Other Connections: Take time to focus on the business and marketing skills in the last few steps. Look at examples of how similar products are marketed. Make a list of the most appealing features that each product advertises.

23 CLASS SCIENCE CHANNEL

This extended project-based learning opportunity can be used with any science concept you teach this year. Kids love watching videos on YouTube, and educational videos made for kids by kids are becoming increasingly popular. Create a YouTube channel for your students to demonstrate different science concepts, and you will increase buy-in in your lessons all year long!

Spotlight on: Any science concept

Driving question: How can we teach people around the world about the awesome power of science?

Audience: YouTube viewers interested in science

PROCESS

1. Introduce the concept by showing a science video on YouTube that was made by kids. Most of your students will be very familiar with this platform already. Tell students that you, as a class, will be working on small hands-on demonstration videos throughout the year to teach others about different science concepts that the class learns about.

2. Work as a class to come up with a catchy name for your YouTube channel. Design a logo and any graphics needed for your channel. Bring in a friend or community member to work with your students to create these graphics. This will create the buy-in for this venture.

3. Using student input, create a video outline template. This is where students will plan videos out before recording them. Having students help create the form will allow them to understand how the process works.

4. Teach your first science concept. Use a variety of hands-on activities and in-depth inquiries. Make sure students take quality notes. Stress the importance of doing so for when they plan out their first video.

5. Split students into groups of four or five. Mix ability levels and interests. Have each group brainstorm ideas for how they want to represent this science concept in a video.

6. Use the video template to plan out the videos.

7. Show students how to use the filming equipment you have available. Most classes start by recording with a cell phone or tablet. Test different filming locations and settings to make sure that they have the clearest video and audio before beginning.

8. Prepare all materials for filming. Have each group film their video in one take. Don't let students continuously start over, because they will end up recording forever for a perfect take. Encourage them to clap twice when they make a mistake so that they can see which parts they need to take out in editing.

9. Have students work together to edit and put the finishing touches on their videos.

10. Upload the best video, or upload all videos to the channel. You will have to decide as a class how you want to handle this. You may also decide to fuse all the videos together as one video, especially if your groups made very short videos.

11. Follow this process for other concepts you learn throughout the year.

Other Connections: Have students fundraise to get more advanced recording equipment such as different cameras, microphones, and editing software. This will provide them with some very important 21st-century skills! You can also easily incorporate speech standards by teaching students how to best present their information.

24 TOOLS FOR CLEAN WATER

Clean water is probably something that your students don't even think about. They have access to water that is already purified and safe for drinking. This project will open their eyes to the process of making water safe to drink.

Spotlight on: Water purification

Driving question: How can we purify water to make it safe to drink for people that don't have access to safe drinking water?

Audience: People without safe drinking water

PROCESS

1. Begin by discussing how your local tap water is purified before it reaches the faucet. If you can, take a field trip to the local water treatment plant to see this process firsthand.

2. Research the difference between safe drinking water and water that is not safe to drink. Discuss the effects of toxins in the water. This would be a great time to read about how tap water contaminated with lead has affected communities.

3. Research different water-filtering systems. Discuss the benefits of each.

4. Have students work in small groups to research easy ideas for filtering water that could be used anywhere, by anyone, with simple materials. There are many ideas online, including several that only use a soda bottle, rocks, sand, cloth, and charcoal.

5. Have each group choose an idea and work together to build a water filter. Take photos and videos of the process. Have them write down each step as they do it, so that they can easily share the process later.

6. Have them test their water filters by adding water from a local, unfiltered water source. Use a digital water-quality tester to easily test the results before and after the water has gone through their filter.

7. Once water quality has been tested and is confirmed as drinkable, have each group work together to create directions for people to make their own. Their end products can use any media; pamphlets and videos are the most common.

8. Determine where this information is needed and how to share it. Making safe water kits would be a great service project!

Other Connections: Connect this project to the Earth's Systems standards by learning about the distribution of saltwater and freshwater on Earth.

25 PLAYGROUND IMPROVEMENT

Many of the best pieces of playground equipment use simple machines. In this project, your students will design fun and functional playground equipment using what they learn about simple machines.

Spotlight on: Simple machines

Driving question: How can we use simple machines to improve the playground for students?

Audience: Students

PROCESS

1. Visit your playground. Have students make a list of their favorite things about the playground. Discuss how to improve the playground.

2. Have students research playground equipment that uses simple machines. Provide them with research materials that include images of different types of simple machines.

3. Task students with designing a new playground that the students in your school would love. Have them incorporate the existing equipment and at least one of each type of simple machine: pulley, wheel and axle, lever, wedge, inclined plane, and screw. Have students work in groups of four.

4. Set up students to design the new playground on paper or devices. Make sure each student is responsible for a part of the design. Take the class to the playground often so that they can see the existing equipment and layout for their designs.

5. Have each group get feedback from students of different ages and revise several times. Then, have groups use household materials to build the playground design.

6. Display the playground designs. Have students from other classrooms do a gallery walk of the playground designs and give reviews. This is a great way for your students to get feedback before submitting their final designs.

7. Have students submit final group designs with individual essays explaining the feedback they received from other students and how they incorporated that feedback, and knowledge of simple machines, into their designs.

Other Connections: Connect to other subject areas by having students raise money for a playground project. They can try to add a piece of equipment to your current playground, or improve a community playground. For this connection, they will need to research the costs of what they want to do and create written material to advertise their fundraiser.

CHAPTER 4

MATH AND FINANCIAL LITERACY

26 DESIGN A MATH GAME

Many students struggle with the basic math facts that are necessary to complete most project-based learning math activities. This project is a great way to teach your students about the structure of project-based learning while helping them learn their math facts!

Spotlight on: Math facts

Driving question: How can we create a math game to help our group and other students practice math facts?

Audience: Students learning math facts

PROCESS

1. Determine which math facts you want students to focus on. This project can be as narrow as the multiplication facts for 9 or as broad as multiplication and division facts for 0 through 12.

2. Begin by putting out a few board games for your students to try out. Spend an hour playing different types of games designed for kids. This will get your students excited about the project while giving them some inspiration for their own games.

3. Discuss the games as a class. Make a list of the parts of the games that students enjoyed the most. Keep this list on the board for students to see when creating their own games.

4. Split students into groups of three. Task students with creating a game that practices certain math facts. Provide them with a list of the facts you want them to use in their games. When they're deciding on the premise of their games, allow students to use the board games they practiced with or make their own boards from scratch. This is an easy way to differentiate: Some groups will struggle with coming up with a game from scratch, while others will enjoy the challenge.

5. After groups brainstorm ideas for their games, have them sketch out their first design. Give them an opportunity to get some feedback from other students and revise their initial design.

6. Work as a class to create an ordered task list of things to do to create their games. Each group will also have their own task list that they can add specific steps to. A couple examples of items on the task list should be "design game pieces" and "write directions."

7. Have each group begin to design their game, including game pieces and answer sheets. After they are finished, have them test the game with other students. Once their games have been tested and revisions have been made, have each group work to write directions for the game.

8. Test the directions. Other students should be able to read the directions and play the game without confusion. This is the most difficult piece. A lot of revision will take place during this step.

9. Play the games! Have students create a box or container for each game, and store all games in a specific area of the classroom. This will allow students to come borrow games anytime they have free time to practice their math facts.

Other Connections: Discuss text features and text structure as students write the directions for their math games. Show students examples from different games to help support the idea that text features make it easier for people to read and understand the game directions.

27 PITCH A PRODUCT

Encourage innovation with this popular project-based learning activity. Your students will work together to make an infomercial-worthy product that solves a common problem.

Spotlight on: Decimal operations

Driving question: How can my team create a product that will solve a common problem?

Audience: Consumers

PROCESS

1. Begin by showing videos of infomercials on YouTube. There are quite a few funny ones that will really engage your students! Discuss the problem that each product solves.

2. Have students brainstorm some common problems that don't yet have a product that offers a solution. Work together as a class to make a "Top 10" list of most interesting problems.

3. Form small groups based on which problem each student is interested in. I prefer to do it this way instead of assigning groups first so that students end up working on a project they're interested in.

4. Tell each group to brainstorm ideas for products that will solve their chosen problem. Groups should have at least three options.

5. Have students create a "market survey" and poll potential consumers to determine which of their product ideas people like the best. Consumers can be other students, school staff members, parents, or community members.

6. Have each group make a prototype of their product. They should keep a record of the cost of each material they use in their product. Provide them with a few online store options they can use to find the cost of materials if they do not purchase materials themselves. If they use an item that comes in a pack, like a sheet of paper, they will have to divide the total price by the number of pieces in the pack to find the cost of the single item they're using. This is great practice for decimal division.

7. Have students work on their prototypes. They should get critique and revise their products several times. Once their prototypes are finalized, have students total up their cost required to make each item. They can also brainstorm ways to keep the price down by substituting lower-cost materials.

8. Help students set prices for their products. Have them get out and do another "market survey," asking their audience what they would be willing to pay for the product. Their goal is to set a price that people would be willing to pay, but also would maximize profit.

9. Have students calculate profit by subtracting the cost of materials from the price they will sell the product for. You can also have them calculate the profit if they sell 50, 100, 500, or 1,000 units.

10. Have your groups create an infomercial for their products using their prototypes, highlighting the price and how to purchase it. Remind them to start by stating the problem and then telling their audience about the solution in an engaging way.

Other Connections: Add a literacy component to this project by sharing books about entrepreneurship with your students. There are many titles to choose from, but my favorites are *Be a Young Entrepreneur* by Adam Sutherland and *Whoosh!: Lonnie Johnson's Super-Soaking Stream of Inventions* by Chris Barton.

28 PRODUCT PACKAGING

This is one of my favorite project-based learning activities for product marketing. It focuses on volume, a skill that students often struggle with because they don't understand the real-life applications. Use this project as an extension of the Pitch a Product project on page 86, or begin a new standalone project.

Spotlight on: Volume

Driving question: How can we design packaging for a product that will convince someone to buy it?

Audience: Consumers

PROCESS

1. Bring in a variety of products of different shapes and sizes. These don't need to be new items; they can be interesting or weird items you have at your house or in the classroom. Divide students into groups of two or three. Assign each group a random item. If extending the Pitch a Product scenario, the students will use their own products.

2. Teach your students the concept of volume as it relates to packaging their products. You will want to bring in different size boxes for students to practice measuring, identifying the length, width, and height, and finding volume. Students can also use these boxes to estimate the size needed for their own packaging dimensions.

3. Have students measure a box around their product to help estimate the required dimensions and volume of the box they will use as packaging.

4. Have students do in-depth research about different types of product packaging. They can do this in a variety of ways, in and out of the classroom. Task students with looking at similar products when they go to the store with their family, taking notes on size and style of the packaging. They can also look through paper and digital advertisements to get ideas.

5. Begin designing product boxes on paper. Have students bring in cardboard, plastic, or other supplies that they can cut and put together to make their own packaging.

6. Once the designs have been perfected, have the groups move on to creating the prototype of their design.

7. Test the packaging with the product. Alter the dimensions if needed. Measure the volume inside and decide what to do with any "wasted" space inside the packaging. Each group will need to do quite a bit of problem solving to figure out how to secure the product snugly in the box.

8. Have each group present their product to a panel of potential consumers. This can be school staff members, parents, students, or community members.

9. After their presentation, have students write a reflection and a summary of what they learned about volume during this project.

Other Connections: Discuss persuasive techniques when preparing students to do their presentations. Help them come up with phrases to say that will sell their product and product packaging to this audience.

29 FLEXIBLE SEATING

Flexible seating is a popular way to give students more independence in the classroom. The downside is that flexible seating can be a big expense and a lot of work for the teacher. Give your students the responsibility of creating and maintaining flexible seating in the classroom!

Spotlight on: Decimal operations

Driving question: How can we use flexible seating to improve our classroom work environment?

Audience: Classroom members

PROCESS

1. Show students photos of flexible seating in other classrooms. Have students discuss what they notice about the flexible seating options.

2. Tell students that they will be planning to get the materials necessary for flexible seating, setting it up, and creating rules and procedures to maintain it. As a class, make a list of flexible seating options that your students would like to have.

3. Divide students into small groups and have them each research one flexible seating option. Have the students determine the cost of the seating, where it will go in the classroom, and what rules and procedures they will need for it.

4. Have all students come back together as a class and draw a layout that uses each group's plan for flexible seating. Incorporate each group's ideas into the classroom layout.

5. Work as a class to calculate the total cost for all pieces. Create a spreadsheet that shows each individual item and the total.

6. Have the groups work together to decide how they will get each type of flexible seating into the classroom. You may want to research grants, fundraise, or create a presentation for the Parent Teacher Organization (PTO).

7. Create all materials necessary to put your plan into action.

8. While waiting for funding and the seating to arrive, have students work together to create rules and procedures for each flexible seating type. They can hang posters that state the rules in each area, or make a digital presentation.

9. Once you get your seating items, have students help put them together and start using them. You will find that your students will treat this seating as a privilege after working so hard for it!

Other Connections: Have students write persuasive pieces that explain how flexible seating will help them be better students. You can use this to persuade the PTO, or other donors, to help fund this project.

30 START A BUSINESS

It's important for students to know the basics about business. In this PBL activity, students will learn business skills while getting the chance to be creative and innovative. You'll be amazed at the business plans your students come up with!

Spotlight on: Decimal operations

Driving question: How can I start a profitable business that will benefit our local community?

Audience: Local investors

PROCESS

1. Have students brainstorm a list of local businesses that their family visits frequently. Have them discuss and write about what they like best about each business. Ask students to reflect on what service or product the business provides the local community.

2. Make a "Top 5" list of the most visited local businesses. Critique each business, identifying how they make money, what they provide to the local community, and what they do better than other similar businesses.

3. Discuss the balance that businesses must have between making profit and helping others.

4. Tell students that they will be working in pairs to create a business plan for a small business that will benefit their community. Have students brainstorm the services and products that are needed in the local community, but not provided by any business yet.

5. Have students research some of the ideas on their list. Have each pair choose an idea to build a business around.

6. Work as a class to create a to-do list for starting a business. Have each pair assign one person as the CEO (leader) and CFO (financial/math person). They will need to assist each other with both leadership and math tasks, but it will help them divide up some of the work.

7. On their task list, make sure that students list items like renting a space, buying furnishings, stocking product, and other tasks that involve money. During these tasks, you will facilitate adding, subtracting, multiplying, and dividing decimals (money). They will probably also come up with tasks like hiring employees and advertising. Determining profit should be a key item on their task list. Before partners begin to work on determining profit, do a mini-lesson on what profit is and how to calculate it. I like to bring in an ad from a store to show the amount the store earns from each item's purchase and a wholesale printout or catalog showing what they pay for the item. If their business provides a service instead of physical products, they will have to calculate the supplies they use to perform this service and any other office costs.

8. Have students work through their task list, doing one thing at a time to prepare for their new business. Once they've thoroughly researched all tasks on their list, have students create a business plan. Give them a format that includes a paragraph on each of these points:

- A description of the business, including the name and purpose

- What their business will do to provide value to the community

- Where their business will be located and what it will physically look like

- What each partner will do as a part of the company

9. Conclude by having students write a persuasive letter to fictitious potential investors, explaining why they should invest money to help them start this business. I often show my students episodes from the show *Shark Tank*, and they write their letters to one of the sharks. Tell them to focus on profit and serving the community. Attach this letter to their business plan and all calculations they have done to prepare for starting their business.

Other Connections: Have students read business-related news articles. I find kid-friendly articles about current events on www .newsela.com. If you have students read about the argument many states are having about minimum wage, you can also tie opinion writing into the topic.

31 FAMILY ROAD TRIP!

This project-based learning activity makes a fantastic home connection. Students will plan out a road trip to take with their family. They'll use their dream destinations and learn about new places in the process.

Spotlight on: Multiplication and division

Driving question: How can I plan a road trip that everyone in my family will enjoy?

Audience: Family members

PROCESS

1. What's a road trip? Kick off this project by showing students photos from one of your family vacations. Discuss the reasons that families travel together.

2. Tell students that they will be planning a road trip for their family. They will need to decide what time of year to go on the trip, as well as the length of the trip. They may have to change these choices as the project progresses to best accommodate their destinations and the other choices that they make.

3. Print out a blank map of the US for each student. Have students make a list of destinations they'd love to visit, research where each place is located, and label each on their map in pencil. You can get atlases from the library or have students use their devices to find this information.

4. Tell students that they will need to narrow down their destinations to match the length of trip they want. They can use a variety of different tools to calculate driving times between each destination. Have students get feedback on their routes before finalizing them.

5. Once they've finalized their routes and trip lengths, it's time to start planning! They will need to create a schedule for each day that includes driving, activities, and accommodations. They need to know the total cost for any activities or lodging accommodations.

6. Model for students how to calculate the total cost of an activity when the price is listed per person. There may also be a different price for kids. They will have to do quite a bit of multiplication and addition during this stage. Students can create tables to help organize the costs for each destination, or they can create spreadsheets on their devices.

7. Students should use their maps to support their schedules. Have them draw a line from location to location and write the travel times. You can also have them calculate the number of miles and the cost of gas to travel those miles. They can work with their parents to figure out the gas mileage that their family car gets. If they don't have a family car, they can research how to rent a car that gets good gas mileage!

8. The end product of this project should be a presentation that each student can give to their family about their trip. It should include all their plans and the total trip cost. Students may use slideshows, posters, animations, or any other media that will engage their audience.

Other Connections: Studying the different states in social studies? Have students research the state capitals and fun destinations in each state.

32 KID-FRIENDLY MENUS

Who better to create a kid-friendly menu than an actual kid? In this activity, students will work with a local restaurant to design a kid-friendly menu that includes the foods they're most interested in.

Spotlight on: Adding money

Driving question: How can I turn a local restaurant's menu into a kid-friendly menu that will help kids order their own meals?

Audience: Local restaurant owners

PROCESS

1. Make connections with local restaurants. You can choose to work with just one restaurant for your entire class, or work with multiple restaurants so that each student group has a different restaurant partner. The benefit for local restaurants is that they will create kid-friendly menus that they can actually use, and the kids and their families will become more familiar with the restaurants. You'd be surprised how many local restaurants do not have a kid's menu.

2. Have the restaurant owner(s) come to your class and tell your students that they are looking for help creating a kid-friendly menu. They should tell students they want it to include food from their adult menu that kids would like, as well as easy-to-understand directions and illustrations.

3. Get a few copies of the adult menus for the restaurant(s) you are working with. Divide students into groups to analyze the menu(s).

4. Start by having students make a "yes" and "no" list of the foods they think should be on the kid's menu. Each group should end with one list that they have all agreed upon.

5. Have students discuss what needs to be on their kid-friendly menu. They should be prepared to include a kid-friendly description, prices, and illustrations. Have them suggest lower prices for a smaller kid's portion. They should use decimal amounts or whole numbers, depending on what's appropriate for your grade level.

6. Have students design and create the kid-friendly menu. After receiving feedback from classmates, have them make revisions. Have them submit a draft to the restaurant owner(s) for further feedback.

7. Have students create their final menus. If you have the technology to do so, have them use an app or software to digitally design the menu for a more professional appearance.

8. After presenting the final menu to the restaurant owner(s), have students use the menus to practicing adding money. You can push desks together to make tables and put tablecloths over them. Then display the menu created by one of the student groups. Have students sit down and "order" from a waiter. Then have the "waiter" calculate the total bill by adding up each person's order cost.

Other Connections: Another math standard that can be connected to this activity is percentages. Have students calculate the tax for their bill using your local tax percentage. This is more appropriate for the older grades, but it doesn't hurt to introduce it to students in a younger grade using calculators to find the tax amount and tip.

33 FAMILY COOKBOOK

This versatile project is a family favorite! You can make a holiday cookbook, a summer cookbook, or a cookbook of special recipes as a gift for Mother's or Father's Day.

Spotlight on: Fractions

Driving question: How can I create a cookbook for my family members to use for years to come?

Audience: Family members

PROCESS

1. Decide what the theme of your class' cookbooks will be. You can choose the theme in advance or have your students come up with ideas and vote.

2. Have students bring copies of family recipes from home. I suggest sending home a letter explaining the project and attaching a few recipe cards so that parents or students can easily copy down recipes in the same format. I also ask for donations of a variety of kitchen measuring tools.

3. Make lots of copies of the recipe cards you get back. You can also add your own recipes or recipes you find online.

4. Have students get into small collaborative groups. They can move their desks together or work at a table. This will also make it easier because you can throw a bunch of the recipes in the middle of the table for them to share. They will create their cookbooks individually, but it's important to have other students to get ideas from.

5. Tell students that they will choose their favorite recipes to put into a cookbook. Have them look through the recipe cards and make a list of the ones they would like to include. Most students will pick familiar foods or recipes with ingredients that they like.

6. Over the next couple of weeks, have students work on their recipe books. Encourage them to try the recipes at home with their family and take photos for their books. Depending on school policies, take your class to the cafeteria to make some of the recipes.

7. During this time, practice using measurement tools in class. Discuss how to change recipes for service size, beginning with doubling a recipe. This is a great way to experiment with real-life addition, subtraction, multiplication, and division of fractions.

8. Have students choose how they want to put their books together. They can type and print, write on larger paper, or make digital cookbooks. If they can't get photos of their recipes, they can create illustrations. Give students plenty of time to create.

9. Have students take home their completed cookbooks to share with their families.

Other Connections: Integrate writing standards by having students write an introduction to their cookbooks.

34 PERSONAL BUDGETING

This budgeting project is one that will stick with your students well into their adult lives. Many adults don't know how to create a budget, but your students will at the end of this engaging activity.

Spotlight on: Decimal operations

Driving question: How can I create a balanced personal budget for my future self?

Audience: Self, family members

PROCESS

1. Hold a discussion about money and budgeting. Ask students what they see their parents doing at home. Discuss ways that students see their parents trying to save money, like using coupons at the grocery store.

2. Send home a letter telling parents about this project. Explain how they can help support the project at home by including their child when paying bills and discussing the family budget.

3. Begin by having each student choose the career they want to pursue when they're an adult. Have them research the average starting salary for that career and write it down. Have students take that salary and divide it by 12 to get their monthly salary.

4. Teach your students about taxes and help them calculate a simple estimation of taxes. I usually have my students estimate that 30 percent will come out of their monthly income for taxes. To calculate taxes in this manner, students will multiply their monthly income by 0.30 to find out how much they will pay. Then, they will subtract the estimated taxes from their monthly income.

5. Have students brainstorm the monthly expenses they will need to plan for in their budgets. Have students make a "needs" and "wants" list.

6. Have students start researching the costs of the items on their "needs" list. These will be things like a home, transportation to work, and food. I encourage students to bring in receipts from their family grocery trips so that they can make an estimation for their food budgets.

7. After students find the cost of each item on their "needs" list, have them subtract it from their monthly income. If they find that they run out of money, they will need to go back and make changes in their budgets. Rent is usually what causes the most problems, but your students will come up with smart solutions, like finding a roommate to split the cost.

8. Have students place at least 10 percent aside for savings before moving on to their "wants."

9. Have students do the same process for their "wants" list as they did for their "needs" list. Entertainment and travel often fall into this category. They will need to research each item on their wants list and subtract it from their budget.

10. Finally, have students put together a portfolio displaying their budgets. They can also include specific information about the home, car, pet, and anything else they chose to put in their budget.

11. Have students present their budgets to their families. Tell them to explain what they learned about budgeting and how it will help them be responsible adults in the future.

Other Connections: This project connects very well with the College Application project (page 188). You can easily use this project to begin a discussion about salaries for different careers and how much college tuition costs for those career tracks at their chosen colleges.

35 DREAM HOME

This PBL activity gets family involved in the process of designing a beautiful dream home. Your students will love all the choices they have during this activity. This project is even better if you find an architect in your community that is willing to come talk to your students about the career.

Spotlight on: Area and perimeter

Driving question: How can I design a dream home that includes all my family's wants and needs?

Audience: Family members, peers

PROCESS

1. Have students draw and describe the home that their family currently lives in. Have them brainstorm a list of things that would make their house better. This could be extra bedrooms, a backyard, a newer kitchen, a pool, or anything they would love to have in their home.

2. Share and discuss their improvement lists. Have students add to their lists if they come up with another idea during discussions.

3. Send students home to ask each family member what they want to add to the improvement list. Students will need to accommodate each family member's wants and needs when designing the home.

4. Have students research the items on their improvement list and save pictures of their favorite solutions. Create a class inspiration board using these pictures.

5. Introduce students to the methods architects use when drawing floor plans for homes, including scale. Show lots of examples, using images online and/or architecture books. Tell students that they will be making their own floor plans. Create a sample floor plan based off of your dream home. If using standard graph paper, they will be using a 1/48 scale (¼ in. = 1 ft.) when they draft their dream home layouts, so each square on the graph paper will represent 1 sq. ft.

6. Use your sample floor plan to demonstrate how to calculate perimeter and area of each room and the entire home. Measure your classroom to find the total area so that students can visualize how large a room of that area is. Discuss how knowledge of area and perimeter are important when looking at a floor plan.

7. Have students begin the first draft of their dream home, using a pencil and graph paper or an engineering graph pad.

8. Keep out all of the sample floor plans and any other resources your students will need while designing their home. If you were able to connect with an architect in your community, have them come in and give feedback on the designs. Have students continually get feedback from their peers and family, and then revise their designs.

9. Remind students to continually check the area and perimeter of each room they're designing to make sure it makes sense. For example, if one of the needs on their list was more cabinet space, they will need to make sure the room has a large area and long walls allowing for lots of cabinets.

10. When students get close to completing their floor plans, bring in paint samples and other home design items. Many home improvement stores will allow you to borrow flooring and tile samples, or donate old ones. They are very generous when it comes to helping students, just ask!

11. Have students finalize their layouts and create drawings to show what some of their rooms will look like. They will use their layouts, drawings, paint samples, inspiration boards, and anything else they want to include for their final product.

12. Display the finished designs for families to view.

Other Connections: Although we focus on area and perimeter for this project, you can incorporate a lot of other math skills. For example, have students research the average cost per square foot of homes in your area, then find out how much their home would cost.

36 ACCESSIBLE WATER PARK

Kids love helping other kids, and this project-based learning activity allows your kids to come up with innovative ideas when they design their own accessible water park.

Spotlight on: Measurement

Driving question: How can we design a water park that is accessible and fun for kids with disabilities?

Audience: Kids with disabilities and their families

PROCESS

1. My favorite example to start this project with is the water park Morgan's Inspiration Island. This water park's attractions are all wheelchair accessible, and guests with special needs are admitted at no cost. Use this example to start a discussion with your students about their friends and family members that have disabilities, and which everyday tasks are difficult for them.

2. Discuss ways you can make a place wheelchair accessible. Have students research how wide walkways and doorways need to be in order to accommodate wheelchairs. Discuss the different ways this can be used to make a water park accessible, such as making it easier to get in and out of restrooms and access other water park features.

3. Arrange students in groups of three or four and help them set up the layouts for their water parks. Mix students with different interests. Have them tape together six to ten sheets of standard size graph paper in any configuration they'd like to represent their accessible water park's property.

4. Have each group of students brainstorm their favorite park rides and features. Have them choose one ride or feature at a time and brainstorm ways to alter the design to make it wheelchair accessible or more appropriate for someone with another disability. An example might be to include verbal cues to help a blind child navigate through a particular area.

5. As students begin to choose their favorite rides and make modifications, have them graph the location on their graph paper. Tell students they will be using a 1/48 scale (¼ in. = 1 ft. on standard graph paper) when they draft their layout, so each square on the graph paper will represent 1 sq. ft. Make sure that they keep this scale in mind when designing walkways, entrances, and other elements of the park. They need to incorporate the measurements they found were wide enough for wheelchairs to pass through.

6. Have students practice measuring the actual width of tables and desks in the classroom to estimate the size of certain pieces in their water parks.

7. To add to their projects, have them sketch out what each ride or water park feature looks like, labeling the parts that make these features accessible. Have students work together to take the sketches one step further by adding color and more details.

8. Have students get feedback on their initial plans from kids with disabilities or their family members. Incorporate feedback into design revisions.

9. Once the final designs are ready, present the water park layout and ride designs to an audience of people with disabilities and their families. Create a book, or an online collection, to share the individual ride ideas.

Other Connections: Make this project come to life by designing a field day for students with disabilities and putting the design into action. Have your students measure and create stations (with and without water) that are appropriate for students with a variety of disabilities. Talk to your local Special Olympics volunteers for help getting this project off the ground.

37 TRAVEL ABROAD

There are so many amazing sights to see when you travel abroad. In this activity, students will have the opportunity to plan a trip for themselves to another country using real-life math skills.

Spotlight on: Addition and subtraction

Driving question: How can I plan a trip for just myself that will allow me to learn more about another country, while staying within my budget?

Audience: Self

PROCESS

1. Borrow international travel books from your local library. You can also put together and share a collection of travel commercials online. Many countries have commercials to encourage tourism, like the "Come to Jamaica" campaign.

2. Have students discuss their options and each choose a country they would like to visit. They can choose to visit additional countries near their first choice later in their project if they'd like, but they need a country to start their trip in. Students that choose the same country can plan and collaborate, but they should also get feedback from other students as they make choices.

3. Set the budget. Your budget depends on the level of your students. I recommend using $5,000 or $10,000 to allow students to have enough money to research and plan for an extended amount of time. Calculators can be used as a modification for students not ready to subtract from an amount this large.

4. Set a trip length. Let your students discuss it as a group and agree on how many days their trips need to be. I recommend a trip of at least 10 days.

5. Have students print or draw a map of the country they're visiting. If they plan on visiting multiple countries, have them print a map of that region. Label the airport and then research the cost of a flight.

6. Have students record the cost of the flight and subtract it from their budget. If the price includes change and your students are not ready to subtract with decimals, have them drop the change. Do the same process with any other transportation costs, including a shuttle or bus from the airport to their hotel, when they choose one.

7. Have students choose activities for each day of their trip. Help them create a template for their itinerary and add travel and activities to each day. Remind them to record all costs and subtract from their budgets.

8. Students should research and make hotel choices. They may choose to stay at a central hotel the entire time, or stay at several different hotels as they travel.

9. Students should budget for food. Have them research the different types of food in the region and the average cost of a meal.

10. Have students make a list of what they will need for this trip, including a passport, luggage, and an international cell phone plan. Students should record these items and subtract their costs from the budget.

11. If students run out of money in their budget before including every necessary expense, have them go back and revise their choices.

12. For their final products, have students put together a travel plan that includes their complete itinerary and tells about the area they are visiting. Give them a choice in how they present this plan. They can create a travel scrapbook, a multimedia presentation, etc.

Other Connections: Make connections to geography and social studies by making detailed maps of each region and writing about the history of the regions. Include writing by having students create travel blogs. Have them pretend that they went on the trip and journal about each day.

38 **DINNER PARTY**

This flexible activity can be used to plan any type of holiday or family dinner. The most popular way it's used in the classroom is to plan a family Thanksgiving dinner.

Spotlight on: Units of measurement

Driving question: How can I plan a dinner party for my friends and family that has just the right amount of food?

Audience: Friends and family

PROCESS

1. Pick up copies of grocery store circulars before beginning. You can use online circulars as well, but there's something about holding paper ads that makes it even more realistic.

2. Tell students that they will be planning a dinner party. You can set a holiday theme or have them pick their own theme. Have them create a guest list of friends and family that they would want to invite to their dinner party.

3. Have students brainstorm a list of foods they would like at their dinner party. Facilitate discussion and help students narrow down their list to a couple of main dishes, several side dishes, and beverages.

4. Discuss serving size. Give some examples of food at dinner parties and have students estimate how many people each food item will serve. A good example would be a turkey: A good rule of thumb is 1 lb. per person. That means that if one of their main dishes is turkey and they are having 10 guests, they will need a 10-lb. turkey. You can find charts and information for how much to buy of different food items online.

5. Teach students about the different units of measurement they will see when looking at dishes and their serving sizes. Your students will likely see pounds and ounces the most, but they may also encounter grams, cups, and inches (pie, for example) on serving size charts. Give students visual examples of the size of each unit.

6. Help students begin to create their shopping lists. This process takes a lot of discussion and critical thinking. They will need to find the serving sizes of specific items in charts online, or estimate by gathering information from friends and family. They will also need to consult the grocery circular or website to see what sizes are available for certain items. For example, in the table that follows, the student determined that two boxes of stuffing would be needed for nine guests. She found that boxes of stuffing come standard in an 8-oz. size, and opted to purchase a second box to make sure that she had enough stuffing even though she only needed 9 oz., not the 16 oz. that two boxes provide.

DISH	SERVING SIZE	NUMBER OF GUESTS	AMOUNT TO PURCHASE
TURKEY	1 lb./person	9	One (9-lb.) turkey
STUFFING	1 oz./person	9	Two (8-oz.) boxes
SWEET POTATOES	½ lb./person	9	4½ lb.
PUMPKIN PIE	One 9-in. pie for 5 guests	9	Two 9-in. pies

7. Have students research each individual dish and beverage they will need for their party. If the dish can't be purchased as a whole, as in the examples above, have them gather the recipe and add the list of ingredients to their list. Most recipes note serving size, so they can double or triple to get the correct amount of servings. The best way to organize this information is in a table or spreadsheet, like the one above.

8. Once their lists have been finalized, have them research the cost for each item on their lists. Create another column on the table to record the cost of each item, and then add the individual costs together to find the total cost for all food and beverages.

9. Let students have fun with creating seating arrangements and choosing decorations for their dinner party.

10. Have them put their plans together and create a display for their final products. I recommend having students bring supplies for their displays and setting up their individual desks as their "dinner table." Many students brought tablecloths, plates, food items to display, decorations, and menus. One year, one of my students even created a centerpiece for her dinner table. Another teacher had each student bring in one of their dishes and they all had a potluck the day before winter break.

Other Connections: Science can easily be connected to any cooking project. During this project, have students complete kitchen experiments using the scientific method. This is a great way to extend practice with units of measurement beyond math time.

39 BAKE SALE

This project-based learning activity is an easy service project, and it teaches cooking and measurement skills using a common theme that kids love: bakery food!

Spotlight on: Units of measurement

Driving question: How can we work together to throw a bake sale that will raise money for a charity or classroom/school need?

Audience: Students and family members

PROCESS

1. Work with your class to determine what you want to raise money for. This project can be used to support a charity or someone in need in the community. It can also be used to raise money for something that your class or school needs.

2. Send home a letter to parents that asks for volunteers and tells a little bit about the bake sale and your goals. Have your students help write and design the letters. This project includes a home portion, so it's especially important to communicate with families.

3. Brainstorm ideas for items to sell at the bake sale. Have students create a poll to give to students at recess or before and after school to find out which items are most popular.

4. Narrow down six to ten different baked goods. Have students form small groups of three based on which item they're most interested in planning for and making.

5. Have each group find a recipe for their assigned baked good. Their goal is to find a recipe that has simple ingredients and doesn't involve any special tools.

6. Bring measurement tools into class and practice measuring. Introduce students to a kitchen conversion chart. Teach and practice any related measurement standards that you can connect to this project.

7. If your school allows it, have your students take a tour of the cafeteria kitchen. Discuss the steps for safe food handling. Hand out gloves and hairnets in plastic bags for students to take home, as well as a printout that covers food safety rules.

8. Set the date and time for your bake sale. Connect with parents to discuss the recipes your students have chosen and coordinate who will be able to help make each recipe. The goal is to have each family have a parent help the student make their baked good for the bake sale. This may not be possible for all families, so see if you can team up some students to make an item together.

9. Have students do all the bake sale planning, including making flyers, posters, and decorations. Set prices for each baked good and make signs before the event.

10. At the event, have students collect the money, make change, and keep track of inventory. After the event, calculate the profits and wrap up the project.

Other Connections: Have students research the total cost of all their ingredients, and then use ingredient costs and recipe yields to calculate cost per item. This is a great introduction to unit rates. You can also have students calculate profit per item after they set their prices.

40 CLASS FIELD TRIP

Planning on taking a class field trip this year? Create ultimate buy-in to project-based learning by allowing your students to help choose and plan your local field trip.

Spotlight on: Decimal operations or basic operations

Driving question: How can we plan a local field trip for our class that our teacher will approve?

Audience: Teacher

PROCESS

1. Begin by having students ask you questions about what you're looking for in a field trip. This will help provide students with the project guidelines in an interactive way. Your students may have questions that you didn't even consider.

2. Have students break into pairs and research local field trip opportunities. They should write down a summary for each field trip location that they find.

3. As a class, make one big list of field trip locations. Work together to cross off any locations that don't meet your original criteria, or don't work for the class in some way. Cut the list down to five or six locations.

4. Have students divide themselves into groups based on which location they are most interested in going to. Each group should thoroughly research their chosen location.

5. After students have researched their field trip locations, have them create a schedule for the field trip.

6. Using their schedule, have each group research and calculate costs for all food and activities on the trip. This step involves multiplying a decimal (money) by a whole number (number of students and/or number of adults). You can change this to multiplication of whole numbers by having students round up to the nearest dollar. Have students record the total costs in a table or spreadsheet.

7. If your class will be taking buses, have your district's bus coordinator visit the class to talk about the fees they charge for field trips. Each group can also have some time to share their ideas with the bus coordinator to make sure that their location is easily accessible and close enough to use the school buses. Add the transportation costs to the total field trip cost.

8. Have each group present their ideas to you. You are their primary audience, so they must make sure that they are tailoring their presentation to you if they want their idea to be chosen. I tell my students that I'm willing to go on any field trip as long as they can give me a list of everything they will learn while there.

9. Choose a location from the presentations as a field trip destination. Work together to make an agenda for the trip and figure out other planning details.

Other Connections: Have students write persuasive essays to go with their projects. This is a great way for them to practice persuasive writing and prepare for their actual presentation by writing reasons and evidence geared toward their audience.

41 PHOTOGRAPHY EXHIBIT

This project requires additional equipment, but it's well worth it! Ask parents to donate digital cameras to use, or use student devices if they have tablets or phones with cameras. If you love photography, you can easily take this project even further than the steps below suggest.

Spotlight on: Symmetry

Driving question: How can I use symmetry to compose a photograph for an exhibit?

Audience: Local photographers

PROCESS

1. Make connections with local photographers or photography students. See who would be willing to come teach your students about photography and help with an exhibit. You'll want at least three photographers to work with your students during this project.

2. Show students photographs that have symmetry. You can take some yourself, have the photographers bring some of theirs in, or find some online. Use this opportunity to teach students about symmetry.

3. Have one or more photographers visit and talk to your students about important parts of photography. Have them tie symmetry into composition, if they can.

4. Help students come up with ideas of what they want to photograph. Have them photograph at least three different things that show symmetry. Have them get feedback from other students and one or more of the photographers before choosing their favorite picture and doing their final editing.

5. Complete final editing. Students can change the colors of the photo and crop for best composition. Have them incorporate the feedback they received.

6. Display the photographs in an exhibit in the school. Invite the photographers that participated and other members of the community. If you want, have the photographs judged and winners chosen.

Other Connections: Have your students only photograph things in nature for a quick science connection.

42 GEOMETRY ART EXHIBIT

Get creative with your students during this hands-on geometry experience. This project is open-ended so that you can have students include representations of geometry that best match your standards.

Spotlight on: Geometry

Driving question: How can I create an art piece that incorporates the things I've learned about geometry?

Audience: Friends and family

PROCESS

1. Introduce the idea of an art exhibit. Show examples of art exhibits from around the world. Tell your students when your class exhibit will be and set goals for what they need to do between now and then to prepare their art pieces.

2. Make a list of geometry concepts that you want students to include in their art pieces. Tailor this to the individual geometry standards that you want students to meet.

3. Have students research each geometry concept you discussed. Model how you want them to take notes and draw pictures of each concept in their notebooks. Have them discuss how each concept could be reflected in their art pieces.

4. Once they have researched and can understand each concept, students should sketch a rough design for their art piece. Encourage 3D pieces that incorporate everyday materials. Provide materials like toothpicks, craft sticks, toilet paper rolls, newspapers, paints, and anything else that is easily available. Students can also bring materials from home. Students can create an art piece that uses other types of media, as long as they go beyond a basic drawing.

5. Have students get feedback on their designs and make revisions. Help them create a task list with the different steps they will take to complete their design. Tell them that they also need a materials list to help them gather their materials before beginning.

6. Begin creating art pieces. Have students use the notes from their research to make sure they are best representing each geometry concept.

7. Finalize art pieces. Work together as a class to plan where each project will go in the exhibit.

8. Create flyers to advertise the exhibit. Your students can also put together an exhibit guide for attendees by each writing two or three sentences about their art piece and putting them all together in a guide with a photo of the completed art project.

Other Connections: Write descriptive paragraphs about art projects in the exhibit. Have students practice this writing type with their own art piece, then write another while visiting the art exhibit.

43 ORGANIZE A CONCERT

This quick project is great for the music lovers in your classroom! Your students will learn a lot about what happens behind the scenes when people plan concerts. I suggest partnering with your music teacher or a music group in your town to plan a fun concert for your school as a part of this project. You can go one step further and use this event to raise money for your school or local cause.

Spotlight on: Arrays

Driving question: How can we organize a concert that will allow concertgoers to sit comfortably and enjoy the show?

Audience: Concertgoers

PROCESS

1. Introduce the topic by showing students videos of performers at different size concert venues. Have students estimate how many people are at each concert. Point out any organized seating and areas for standing and dancing.

2. Introduce students to the person or group you are partnering with for this concert. As a class, make a list of questions you want to ask them about their needs for the concert. Have students pair up to practice preparing for this concert.

3. Decide what arrays you want your students to create. Write different numbers on slips of paper. Numbers like 40, 60, 80, and 100 make easy starting places. These are the number of seats your students will arrange in arrays.

4. Give each pair of students a random slip of paper to find out how many people they will have attending their concert. Have the students use graph paper to create an array of seating. Remind them that when they multiply the number of seats in each row by the number of seats in each column, they should get the total number of seats listed on their slip of paper.

5. Have them label the seats (1A, 2A, 3A, etc.) using a numbering system of their choosing that tells both the row and column that the seat is in.

6. Allow students to use art supplies to design a fictitious concert venue around the seating array they have sketched out. Encourage them to research other concert venues to see what other areas they need to plan out. They will want to look at different types of stages and learn what else is commonly found at concert venues.

7. Have each student write a short essay explaining how they arranged their seats and why their venue will provide a comfortable and fun experience for concertgoers.

8. Work together as a class to put together a real concert at your school using what they've learned while creating their fictitious concert venue and seating.

Other Connections: Have a few of your musicians play a small concert in this area to really get a feel for the seating and the venue you've created. This is a great way to bring the musical talents of your students into the project.

44 PLAN A DOG PARK

Whether or not your city has a dog park, this is a great way to get your students interested in the real-world application of the math they're learning.

Spotlight on: Area and perimeter

Driving question: How can we create a functional dog park that both dogs and their owners will enjoy?

Audience: Dogs and their owners

PROCESS

1. Introduce the topic to your students by showing them pictures of a local dog park. It would be even more fun if you could visit one as a class!

2. Have students learn more about different dog park designs by providing them with a list of dog parks to research. Provide an organizer for students to record the common things they notice in each dog park and any unique items they would want to include in their own local dog park.

3. Work as a class to make a list of the essential elements of a dog park. These are things like fences, water, and grass. Talk about the total area of some of the parks you examined, so that students can get a good sense of what the area of a small park would be compared to the area of a larger park.

4. Group students into groups of two or three. Give them graph paper to make an initial draft of their dog park. Discuss scale. Your students will be using a 1/48 scale (¼ in. = 1 ft.) if you use standard graph paper, so each square on the graph paper will represent 1 sq. ft. For a larger area, have students tape multiple pieces of graph paper together.

5. Teach and apply perimeter and area by measuring items that may be found in the dog park. For example, you can take students out to a bench at your school to measure the perimeter, so that they can return to their dog park map and draw benches of the same size.

6. For items that you cannot go out and measure, have students research the sizes online or in a dog park catalog. The Park Catalog company has a printable catalog online (www.theparkcatalog .com), as do a few other companies that sell dog park equipment.

7. When they're finished with their initial designs, have them present to a group of dog owners. This could be parents or staff members that have dogs. Have them get feedback, record the feedback, and use it to make their dog park designs better.

8. After further research and revision, have students finalize their designs. Have them work together to make 3D models of their dog parks, keeping the scale intact.

9. Present final designs by "unveiling" the dog park designs to the same dog park owners that gave feedback earlier in the project.

Other Connections: Use the dog park catalog and other resources to research the total cost of creating the dog park. If you want to use fractions with area and perimeter, show students how to split the squares on the graph paper into fractional pieces.

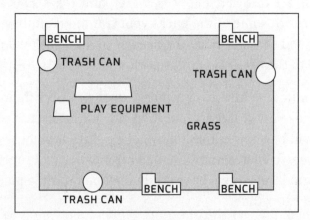

45 THE GREAT OUTDOORS

There's nothing more exciting than a project that gets you outdoors! You can use this scenario to plan for a real class hike, or just use it to share packing information with families new to hiking.

Spotlight on: Volume and weight

Driving question: How can we efficiently pack a bag that will provide all necessary supplies for a 4-hour hike?

Audience: Hikers

PROCESS

1. Before beginning, ask parents to lend you an empty hiking bag, snacks, and some hiking supplies that they use. I suggest also collecting reusable water bottles of varying sizes. You will also need measuring cups with milliliters or ounces labeled (depending on your specific measurement standards). Label all pieces so that you know which item came from which family. You can also get people from a local camping store involved. You're going to want a pack for each group of three students.

2. Split students into groups of three. Show students the hiking bags and make a list of some items that would be important to bring on a hike. Have students research supplies needed for hiking and make separate "necessity" and "luxury" lists. Items having to do with food and water are necessities. Anything extra that would make the hiking trip easier are luxuries.

3. Give each group a random hiking bag. Have students estimate how much they think the bags will weigh when they fill it up.

4. Begin with the most important item: water. Have students do research to answer the question "How much water does each person need to drink while hiking for 1 hour?" Discuss their findings. Use this information to calculate how much water is needed for 4 hours of hiking.

5. Introduce students to volume, using the water as an example. If you have reusable water bottles that have the liquid volume labeled on the outside, that's a great visual for students. However, giving students unlabeled bottles of a variety of sizes will help them learn even more about finding volume.

6. Have students use reusable water bottles and/or plastic water bottles to pack the exact amount of water suggested for 4 hours of hiking into their backpacks. For the unlabeled bottles, have them fill the bottles with liquid, then pour the liquid into measuring cups to find the total volume of water for each bottle.

7. Next, research the amount of food needed and what types of food people take hiking. Bring in a variety of hiking snacks for them to pack.

8. Have students pack any other supplies on their necessities list. Lastly, have them pack what they want from their luxury list, if they have room.

9. Bring in a scale and have students weigh their packs. Have them try walking from one end of your playground to another to make sure they haven't overpacked. If their packs are too heavy, have them take some unnecessary items out, and then weigh and test them again.

10. Have students create a written or video guide instructing other beginning hikers on how to pack for a short hike. Make sure that they discuss the volume of water needed per person, per hour, and how to measure volume to make sure you have enough.

Other Connections: Make science connections by learning more about safe drinking water (see page 79) and how water is filtered. Discuss safety concerns when hiking and talk about what to do if you get lost or need help while hiking.

46 ORIGAMI CREATIONS

Origami is a fun way for your students to get creative, while covering many different geometry standards. It's especially great for your tactile students! I recommend getting 6-x-6-inch origami paper for this project, but it can be done with regular paper.

Spotlight on: Geometry

Driving question: How can we make unique origami creations to brighten someone's day?

Audience: Friends and family

PROCESS

1. Show students a few short YouTube videos on origami to introduce them to the concept. Many students may already be familiar with it.

2. Have each student make a list of five friends and family members that they think could use a day brightener. Discuss, in groups, why they chose these people.

3. Model how to brainstorm the things that each individual person on their list likes. Provide them with several resources to use when they research origami projects that will best fit each of the people they chose. These resources can be origami books, websites, or videos.

4. As a class, dedicate an area of the classroom to 2D and 3D shapes seen in origami projects. The table below shows what it might look like if you had students use a poster to record the different shapes they see while folding. The list of shapes would grow larger as the project went on. Another way you can do this is to have a photo of the shape and have students add their name on a sticky note when they see the shape in their origami. Make sure that students are constantly utilizing this area during the project.

SAMPLE BEGINNING RECORD

SHAPES WE'VE SEEN IN OUR ORIGAMI	
RIGHT TRIANGLE	Jared, Mica, Jazeel
DIAMOND	Darlene, Jose
CUBE	Mark, Tom, Cari, Seth

5. As students build their origami projects, teach them about shapes and angles. Have them unfold one of their origami projects and label and record the different angles they folded.

6. Have students work until they have five different origami gifts that are personalized for the five people they chose.

7. Have students continue to measure the angles inside of their creations and leave a nice little note inside for the person they are giving the piece to.

8. Tell students how you want them to present their gifts. After they have done so, have them write about how each origami piece brightened the recipient's day.

Other Connections: You can easily integrate art and design standards into this project, such as making connections between visual arts and other disciplines. Any art process standards will also fit into this project well.

47 PLAN A BIRTHDAY PARTY

This project-based learning activity can incorporate a ton of important math skills. Because elapsed time is a standard I get asked about a lot, I decided to use it as the main focus of this PBL activity.

Spotlight on: Elapsed time

Driving question: How can I plan a birthday party that keeps all the kids and adults entertained?

Audience: Friends and family

PROCESS

1. Have students share past experiences with their own birthday parties and parties they've attended. Each student should make a list of the things they liked and disliked about the birthday parties they've been to.

2. As a class, make a list of what people do when planning a party. These will be tasks like inviting people, planning food, and planning activities.

3. Ask the question: How long does it take kids or adults to get bored between activities at a birthday party?

4. Teach about elapsed time. Lead a discussion that relates elapsed time to the question in the step above. Have each student decide what the optimal elapsed time between activities should be at their party.

5. Have each student make a schedule of their party's activities, using the increments of time they chose. Some students will want activities to happen more often (e.g., every 15 minutes), while others will want to spend a longer amount of time between activities. Give students ample time to research their activity ideas to make sure they are plausible for their party.

6. Have each student choose and write out the starting time of their party and the time of each activity. Ask questions like: How much time has elapsed between the bounce house and the cake activities? Have students represent their elapsed time between activities on a clock, if necessary.

7. To tie in other math standards, have students research how much each activity will cost. For some activities, they will need an estimate of how many people are attending. Have them add up their individual activity costs to find the total cost.

8. Refer to the list your students made of what people have to do when planning a party. Complete all the activities on the list, from making invitations to planning the food and drinks.

9. Take each student's plan and put it in a binder or small box, to take home to share with their families.

Other Connections: Connect to creative writing by having students write a fictional story as if the party really happened. Have them use details from their plan as the details in their story.

48 WATER CONSERVATION

This project will have long-lasting effects on the way your students think about water usage. Your students will learn the real-life applications of data collection, graphing, and measurement.

Spotlight on: Graphing data

Driving question: How can I create an action plan for my family that will reduce our home water usage by at least 10 percent?

Audience: Family members

PROCESS

1. Discuss the importance of water. My book of choice for starting this discussion is *The Drop in My Drink: The Story of Water on Our Planet* by Meredith Hooper.

2. As a class, make a list of ways you use water at home.

3. Research the average number of gallons of water required for different household functions. For example, how much water is used when you flush a toilet? What about 10 minutes in the shower? Make a table that shows these water-usage facts.

4. Have your students work together to create a water-usage tracking chart for them to use at home over the following week. They should track things like the amount of time spent in the shower, number of toilet flushes, and loads of laundry or dishes. Make sure that their chart can track everyone in their household's water usage and is broken down daily for a weekly total.

5. While students are tracking water usage at home, have them research ways to conserve water.

6. Have students bring in their tracking charts. Use the average water usage table you created to estimate their daily water use, or use an online water use calculator. (www.swfwmd.state.fl.us/conservation/thepowerof10)

7. Help students calculate the total daily and total weekly water usage. Show them how to create a graph showing the daily usage.

8. Analyze the data. Is there a particular day of the week when more water is used? If so, why is this, and how can this information be used to make a conservation action plan?

9. Have students work in groups of two or three to analyze all of their information. Help them identify what activities are using the most water in their individual households.

10. Help students calculate what 10 percent of their total weekly water usage would be. Fifth graders should be able to multiply their weekly usage by 0.10. Lower grade levels can do this with the help of a calculator. This is the number of gallons they need to conserve in order to meet their goal.

11. Have each student begin writing their individual action plans. They can work in groups to get feedback and keep the discussion going. Have them follow these steps:

- Identify goals: Write out how many gallons they need to conserve.

- Create tasks to meet these goals.

- Assign tasks to the people that need to complete them. For example, if Dad takes 15-minute showers, assign him the task of timing his showers so that he only takes 10 minutes.

- Prioritize the tasks by determining which will conserve the most water.

- Choose dates to meet goals and to evaluate the effectiveness of the action plan.

12. Once students are done with drafting their action plans, have them begin a new water usage–tracking chart. Students will need to track water usage following their new action plans for at least a week in order to evaluate effectiveness. Leave it up to your students if they want to implement all of the changes on the first day, or implement a new change each day of the week. Both ways will give very interesting data.

13. Have students add their second week of data to their graph. Have them reflect on the effectiveness of their changes. Did they meet their water-conservation goal?

Other Connections: Make a writing connection by having students write a persuasive letter to their family members explaining why they need this action plan. Have students attach the letter to the action plan and hand it out to each family member. I would also use this project to teach standards about volume and measurement, especially those relating to gallons. You would be surprised how many students don't know what a gallon looks like. They're shocked when they find out how large a gallon is when their family is using thousands of gallons of water!

49 HEALTHY STUDENT LUNCHES

It's a pretty common occurrence to find students that hate school lunch. Help your students understand the rules and guidelines that schools have to follow, while giving your cafeteria manager and principal some student-approved school lunches that meet these guidelines.

Spotlight on: Basic operations (add, subtract, multiply, and divide)

Driving question: How can we plan an affordable, healthy student lunch that students will enjoy?

Audience: Cafeteria manager and principal

PROCESS

1. Before beginning, find out what support you can get from your cafeteria staff and administration. If they're willing to help, you can tour the school kitchen and have the cafeteria manager talk to your students about lunches as a part of your project kickoff.

2. Collect articles for your students to read about school lunches. My favorite resource for this is Newsela (www.newsela.com), which usually has many current articles on what's happening with school lunches.

3. Have students discuss what they like and dislike about school lunches. Have them narrow down the problems to two or three key issues. Taste, choice, and waste are three common concerns that students come up with.

4. Have students research the current guidelines for school lunches. This would be a great topic for the cafeteria manager to discuss with your students. Tie in any health and nutrition standards that address eating a balanced diet.

5. Have students work in pairs to research and plan for one student lunch that meets the guidelines. Have them look closely at the nutritional facts for each item that they want to include in their lunch. This information can often be found online, or students can take a research trip to the grocery store with their families to take photos of nutritional fact labels for the food items in their lunch plan.

6. Discuss serving size and how to calculate it if they need a smaller or larger serving size than what is listed. For example, if one slice of wheat bread has 60 calories, you can multiply it by two to get 120 calories for two slices of bread.

7. Have students create a chart that lists each item in their school lunch and all the nutritional facts for a serving for one student. Have them add up total calories, sugar, sodium, and anything else they need to meet the federal guidelines for student lunches.

8. Facilitate while your students get feedback on their lunches. Have them come up with a way to find out if the people in the school would actually eat them. After they make some revisions, have them finalize their individual student lunches.

9. Have each pair calculate the cost of their lunch by finding the cost of the ingredients. A lot of division will happen during this step. If there are 20 slices of bread in a loaf that's $4.25, then each slice is about $0.21. For the younger grades, have them estimate or use calculators for these tough calculations, or provide them with prices that are easier to calculate.

10. Prepare students to present their lunches to cafeteria staff and administrators. Have them choose how they want to present the information. Remind them to keep their audience in mind. What would these adults like to hear that would convince them to use their school lunch ideas?

Other Connections: Incorporate additional instruction about nutritional facts and serving size in order to integrate more health standards. You can also modify this to make it a service project by planning healthy lunches, then packing these lunches for the local food bank.

50 SAVING FOR COLLEGE

Do your students know what college costs? It's never too early to start thinking about this. This project will help prepare your students and their families for tuition by creating a college savings plan for each student. The bulk of this project can be done with grades 3 through 5, but a few more challenging steps are included at the end to use with older students.

Spotlight on: Multi-digit addition and subtraction

Driving question: How I make a college savings plan that will help me attend my dream college?

Audience: Self and family

PROCESS

1. Reach out to local colleges for informational materials and support. Many colleges will even send a representative to schools to talk about their college. If you reach out far enough in advance, you can also have materials mailed to you from colleges around the country.

2. Lead a discussion about what careers students want when they grow up. Have students do research to find out education requirements for their chosen careers.

3. Research the career programs that your local colleges have. Find two or three other schools around the country that have a degree program for this career.

4. Work as a class to design a table that students can use to organize the college information. Write the college names, degree programs, tuition costs, and dorm housing costs. This will take a bit of research. Students may have to get help contacting a school if this information isn't available in pamphlets or online.

5. Choose a focus: addition or subtraction. To focus on addition, have students add the cost of tuition, dorm, food, and transportation for four years. To focus on subtraction, set a budget and have students subtract the costs from this budget as they calculate them. They'll have to get creative with how they handle some of the costs if you set a budget.

6. Continue to research the costs and organize the information. Food and transportation costs can be estimated in a variety of ways. Have students brainstorm ways to estimate these costs.

7. Have each student pick the college they want to complete their degree program at. Emphasize that it doesn't have to be the cheapest option. There are many questions they should ask to choose the correct college.

8. Help students write out a plan to save money for college. Using the total college costs for four years, have them calculate the amount they would have to save every month beginning today.

9. Attach each college plan and set of calculations to a college and career portfolio students will show their parents. They can make posters, t-shirts, or anything that shows school spirit for their chosen college.

10. Have them present at home, or bring the families in to experience the presentations at school.

Other Connections: This project connects to one of my favorite opinion writing prompts: Should college be free? There are some excellent points on both sides of this argument, and students love debating it!

CHAPTER 5

ENGLISH LANGUAGE ARTS

51 CHILDREN'S BOOKS

Children's picture books have always been a fun way for young kids to learn lessons. During this activity, your students will use their best reading and writing skills to create a children's book of their own.

Spotlight on: Plot and theme

Driving question: How can we portray a theme to teach a young child an important life lesson?

Audience: Young children (ages three to six)

PROCESS

1. Read your favorite picture book to your students. Discuss the themes in this book.

2. Have students brainstorm things that they feel strongly about. Have them include things they've struggled with in their childhoods, like wearing glasses, divorce, not getting along with siblings, etc. Have students choose one of these things to write a children's story about.

3. Pull out your favorite picture book again to discuss plot. Create a plot pyramid and map out the difference pieces of plot.

4. Have students individually brainstorm ideas for a story that teaches young kids about the issue they chose to write about.

5. Facilitate critiques and revisions until each student has a solid idea for their story.

6. Have students map out their story plots. Model how to create a storyboard to help them illustrate the plot.

7. Have students start writing stories using their storyboards. Continue to constantly critique and revise.

8. Once the final drafts are finished, have students format the books and illustrate them. This can be done on paper or on their devices. There are many websites and apps available for creating picture books.

9. Set up a time to take your students to a preschool or kindergarten class. Have each of your students read their book to another student.

Other Connections: Many art standards can be incorporated into the illustration portion of this project.

52 AUTHOR STUDY

One of my main goals has always been to keep students reading. In this simple PBL activity, your class will be filled with a variety of different books!

> **Spotlight on:** Author's craft
>
> **Driving question:** How can we share our favorite authors with other students in order to create a literature-rich school environment?
>
> **Audience:** Students

PROCESS

1. Introduce your favorite children's author. Show students some of the books the author has written and explain what you like most about their writing. Read aloud some excerpts if you have time.

2. Tell students that you want them to think about their favorite authors. If a student doesn't have one, tell them to think about their favorite book. Work with students to help them find information on their favorite authors and books.

3. Send home a letter to parents explaining the purpose of this project and noting which author the child has chosen. Ask for families to provide as many books as they can by this author for their child to bring into class. Include information on obtaining a library card for families that aren't familiar with this process. Work closely with your school librarian or local library to help get books for the students that are unable to bring in books by their author.

4. Once students have a variety of titles by their authors, it's time to do more research. Have students find background information on their authors, including information on their family background and education.

5. Discuss why students think the authors wrote these books, bringing in information about their background to support these discussions.

6. Have each student decide whether to re-read their favorite book by their authors, or read a new one during the project. They can do this at home and/or in class, depending on what works best for your class.

7. Have students create a journal or blog as a way to share their thoughts as they read.

8. While students are reading, facilitate discussions about authors and their craft. Dive into subtopics within author's craft. One example is literary devices. You can have your students search their books looking for common literary devices.

9. As students continue to read, integrate other literature standards. Use mini-lessons and discussion to help students look for these concepts in their books.

10. After a couple of weeks, have students brainstorm a way that they can share about their authors and books. I recommend collaborative sharing instead of a presentation to the class. You might create a bulletin board of suggested reading or a display in the school library. I have also seen students use a collaborative blog or website to share author suggestions and reviews with students in the school and around the world. Support students as they plan and implement their idea.

11. After completing, reflect on what their project did to create a literature-rich environment in their school.

Other Connections: Connect additional literature standards such as theme, setting, and plot by leading discussions using their individual books.

53 GROWTH MINDSET

This PBL activity is a great way to increase positive thinking in your classroom while hitting on an important ELA standard.

Spotlight on: Character traits

Driving question: How can I reflect on character and character traits in a way that will help me grow as a student?

Audience: Self

PROCESS

1. Introduce character traits by making a list of your own. Ask students which actions you take that display each of these character traits.

2. Discuss how people's attitudes and actions help us identify their character traits. Analyze a character from a book you've read recently in class as an example.

3. Read about growth mindset. Have your students make a list of some of the character traits that go along with having a growth mindset.

4. Tell students that you want them to create a reflection journal that they will write in every day. They can choose how to set this up. Some may want to do a private blog while others will want to write in a personal journal.

5. Each day, have students choose a character trait to discuss with a partner. Have them identify if that character trait is helpful or harmful to growth mindset. Have them journal daily about how they feel about their goals and tasks at school and home, keeping growth mindset in mind.

6. After a few weeks of journaling, tell students that they will reflect on their character traits and attitude toward school. Have them create a plan of how they can improve and move toward a growth mindset.

7. Model goal setting and reflection for your students. We can always improve as teachers, and it's important that students see the reflecting we do behind the scenes.

8. Have students create an end product for themselves that displays their goals, what traits they love about themselves, and their plan for growth. These will be personal and will not be shared with other students.

9. Grade based on students' self-reflections and descriptions of what they did.

Other Connections: Use growth mindset and goal setting in all the other subject areas to promote persistence and hard work.

54 CLASSROOM LIBRARY

If you want to build more interest in your classroom library, this is the project for you! Students will work to read and catalog the books in your library, while designing and maintaining a space that encourages reading.

Spotlight on: Genre

Driving question: How can we create a classroom library that makes it easy and fun to find new books to read?

Audience: Students

PROCESS

1. Begin by showing students photos of other classroom libraries. Prep five to ten photos of classroom libraries that seem really fun for kids.

2. Tell students that they will be working together to catalog books and create a better library for the class.

3. Brainstorm a task list as a class. Include tasks that will need to be completed to make your library a reality. There should be tasks related to design, organization, and implementation. The only requirement I give is that the organization system be by genre.

4. Split students up into groups based on the tasks they're most interested in. Within these groups, have students create an action plan and a mission statement that tells the purpose and goal of their specific group. You want each group to have a very specific job during your library project.

5. Have all students begin going through the books you currently have in your library. Discuss genre and look at several examples of each. Work as a class to organize the books into genre. Have all students make a chart or table of books where the genre is on the top and all books in that genre are listed below.

6. While groups are working on their individual pieces, have every student work on reading a book from the library and creating an info sheet on the book for a library book catalog. This sheet should include the title, author, genre, and a brief description. Make a book catalog by laminating every page and adding them to a binder to store in your class library. The group that is tasked with organization can organize this binder and create a cover page.

7. Your class won't be able to read every book during this project, but as the year goes on and they continue to read books from the library, they can write pages for the rest of the books.

8. Work to find funding for any furniture or other items needed for your library. You may also want to have students work on ways to get new books for the library.

9. Bring the groups together and implement the new classroom library. Make sure that at least one group is in charge of organizing the books by genre. They can use the genre lists they created earlier to do this.

10. Enjoy your new library! Encourage students to continue the project throughout the year by regularly improving the library.

Other Connections: Tie in informational writing standards when having students write the info sheets for their book catalog. This would be a great time to discuss writing without personal opinions.

55 SUPPORT A CAUSE

My favorite thing about project-based learning is that it can be used to make a real difference. Having your class support a pressing or timely cause is a great way to teach them about compassion while applying reading and writing skills.

Spotlight on: Informational reading skills

Driving question: How can we learn about and support a cause that will make a difference for a group of people or animals?

Audience: People that may support the cause

PROCESS

1. Share news articles and videos about the cause your class will be supporting. This cause can be something that was discussed in local, regional, or national news. Natural disaster relief, an overflow at the local animal shelter, or a food shortage at the local food bank are common causes that your students can tackle.

2. While reading articles about the cause, incorporate informational reading skills like main idea, text structure, and firsthand vs. secondhand accounts.

3. Have students discuss the main ideas from the text and begin making a list of what items are needed to help this cause.

4. Have students determine what they can do to help. Start with a big goal and then break it into several small things they will have to do to meet this goal.

5. Break students into small groups to work on these smaller tasks. If students decide to do something like a fundraiser or food drive, smaller tasks may be things like creating flyers, organizing the event, and handling/processing money or items collected. Have each small group submit a plan on how they will handle their tasks.

6. Prepare for and implement the plan. Bring in parents and adults from the community to help. If you're helping a local cause, have a representative speak to your students and assist with reviewing their ideas and providing feedback. All products made for a fundraiser or drive should be geared toward its audience: people that would be willing to help support the cause.

7. After your event is over and the local cause has received your class' contributions, reflect on the difference your class made.

Other Connections: Have students write a friendly letter to their friends and family members explaining how they want to support this cause and what people can do to help. Students can print and share this letter or send it as an email to get outside support on this project.

56 **SCHOOL PLAY**

I love incorporating theatre into my reading lessons. Project-based learning is an easy way to use theatre authentically. In this project, students will read and act out plays to learn the elements of drama before producing their own school play!

Spotlight on: Drama

Driving question: How can we produce a play for our school and community?

Audience: School and community

PROCESS

1. Before beginning, discuss this project with your administrators and find people at your school that would be willing to help. Start discussing when it would be best to put on the play for students and teachers. Your PTO, if you have one, may be willing to fund materials for props and help your students organize and advertise the play.

2. Have students watch a children's play and write down what they observe about it. Many local colleges or theatre groups put on children's plays. You can also find some recorded on YouTube.

3. Discuss the elements of drama at length. Have students create posters or make interactive notes to keep track of what each element of drama looks like.

4. Provide students with dramas to read. Look for the elements in both live plays and written dramas. Many textbooks include drama pieces, but you can also find full scripts for children's plays online.

5. Choose a few children's plays that you think would be a good fit for your class. Don't take on any complicated or long plays if you've never helped put on a school play before.

6. Have students read the plays in groups. Continue to solidify their understanding of the elements of drama as they read.

7. After the students have read all the plays, have them vote on their favorite.

8. Brainstorm as a class the steps you will have to take to produce the play for the school. Some important steps are choosing a location, setting a time and date, choosing a cast, practicing, making props, and advertising the play to other students and teachers.

9. Divide up tasks and work as a class to prepare your play. You will probably need to utilize some time at recess or before or after school to practice lines and make props. It's also OK to use classroom time for this as well. In addition to learning about drama and meeting ELA standards, your students will be learning important 21st-century skills while working on this project.

10. Enjoy the results! The parents and students will love watching your children's play.

11. Reflect on the process and have students summarize what they've learned.

Other Connections: After this experience, have students write their own original drama using the elements of drama.

57 MODERNIZE A FAIRY TALE

In this fun activity, students will choose a fairy tale to modernize. The best part of this project is when they work with younger students to get feedback on their new stories!

Spotlight on: Fairy tales

Driving question: How can I make a fairy tale more modern to make it more interesting for kids like me?

Audience: School and community

PROCESS

1. Before beginning, reach out to a teacher with younger students, preferably in kindergarten or first grade. This teacher should be willing to set aside some time to have your students read their stories to their students.

2. Have students read a variety of classic fairy tales to give them some background knowledge. Use this time to discuss the elements of fairy tales.

3. Have students discuss what they like and dislike about each fairy tale. Sometimes we encourage students to like everything they read, but that isn't realistic. Critiquing stories is a great way for them to learn!

4. Split students into groups of three based on which fairy tales they'd like to work with.

5. Facilitate a discussion with your students about what aspects of fairy tales aren't modern or relevant to them and what they can change to make the fairy tales more relevant.

6. Visit your buddy classroom and have your students read the original fairy tales to their buddies. Have each group of your students read to a small group of buddy students.

7. Have your students ask the younger kids what parts of the story they don't understand, and how they can make the stories better. Your students can also share ideas for making the stories better for younger kids.

8. Have students continue the discussion on how they will update their fairy tales. Have them collaboratively make a list of what they need to update in the beginning, middle, and end. Your students may have suggestions like adding technology, making female characters more independent, or updating events from the story.

9. Have students begin a rough draft of their new stories. Within each group, each student should be in charge of writing one piece of the story (beginning, middle, or ending) so that every group member is equally participating.

10. Have students put together their pieces to make one rough draft. Have them return to their buddy classroom to read their stories to the younger students for feedback.

11. After your students get feedback and revise, have them begin writing their final story drafts. This is the step where they begin to create it in book form. This can be done on paper or their devices, if you prefer to have students create ebooks. Make sure that they leave room for illustrations.

12. Have students finalize and illustrate the drafts, then return to the younger students to read their final updated fairy tales.

13. Keep the stories available in your classroom so that students can read the modern fairy tales for years to come.

Other Connections: During the writing portion of this activity, model the writing process for creative narrative writing to show students the real-world applications for this type of writing.

58 FAMILY TREE

This project makes a great home connection. You'll work closely with families when your students tell the story of an older family member's childhood in written and interactive form. The final product will be a part of a large gallery of childhood stories for everyone to enjoy!

Spotlight on: Nonfiction writing

Driving question: How can I tell the story of a family member's childhood?

Audience: Family members and school community

PROCESS

1. Before beginning, video yourself interviewing the oldest relative you have access to. Ask them to tell their best childhood memory and explain what it was like being a kid in the time period they grew up in. Arrange an area where you can display the final products for family members to view.

2. Show your video to your students to introduce them to the project.

3. Have your students brainstorm a list of the oldest relatives that they know. Send home a letter to parents that explains the project. Have students work with their families at home to decide which family member they will be honoring with this project.

4. After students have determined whose life story they will be telling, have them create some interview questions. Model how you came up with your interview questions and explain which ones got the most interesting responses.

5. Critique and revise interview questions. Make sure students have questions that will elicit interesting stories about a person's life. Focus on what it was like being a kid when they grew up, especially the aspects that are different from today's kids.

6. Have students complete their interviews, writing down answers and taking video of the interviews, if they can. Let students know that they will continue to talk to this relative as they write about them.

7. Model your own writing about your relative before students begin theirs.

8. Have students start writing about their relative's childhood. Follow the writing process, beginning at pre-writing, and use this as a way to make it applicable to real-life writing. Make sure to build in time for students to get and share ideas with other students.

9. As students are writing, have them think about an interactive element they can include with their writing. This could be a video or some sort of photo display of their relative's childhood.

10. Students should begin working on the interactive element and revise the written portions.

11. Finalize all work and display it in a gallery for the school and their families to view.

Other Connections: Students will see the differences in the childhood norms of different time periods. You can make a connection to social studies standards by making a timeline of historical events from the relative's childhood.

59 OP-EDS

Make journalists out of your students with this real-life writing activity! Your students will research relevant issues and write their own opinion pieces to submit to the local newspaper.

Spotlight on: Opinion writing

Driving question: How can I write an op-ed for a local newspaper that will convince people in the community to agree with my opinion?

Audience: Local community

PROCESS

1. Reach out to a local newspaper to tell them what you're doing with your class. See if you can get a representative to work with you and your class. The person in charge of the op-ed section of the paper would be the best candidate.

2. Find two articles on a topic: one that is an op-ed (opinion), and the other that is neutral in nature. A great place to find free opinion pieces is Newsela.com. As a class, compare the two articles. Discuss the importance of opinion pieces in news publications.

3. Brainstorm topics with your students. Your students may know quite a few recent issues if their families discuss news around the dinner table. If they don't, you can have students read additional age-appropriate articles about current issues.

4. Make a list of the topics your class discussed. Have each student choose the issue they're most interested in. Students can work collaboratively to research these issues, but have each student produce their own op-ed.

5. Students should begin researching their issues. They should research all sides of the issue and record the facts they learn before forming an opinion. Once they form an opinion, they will need to continue researching for facts that support this opinion.

6. Discuss the format of an op-ed. Read a few more so that students are familiar with what their writing should look like. Have your newspaper contact come in and discuss what they look for in an op-ed when they choose what to publish.

7. Have students begin writing the rough drafts of their op-eds, using the facts from their research to support their opinions. Constantly facilitate discussion, critique, and revision during this step.

8. Have students write final drafts of their op-eds. Submits these to the newspaper representative. It would be great if they were willing to publish a few student op-eds, with parent permission.

9. Publish your op-eds on your class blog or website.

Other Connections: During the research portion of this project, teach your students about credible sources. This is especially important with all the fake news floating around the internet. Students need to support their opinions with proven facts.

60 YOUNG JOURNALISTS

Does it seem like your students and their families don't really read the school calendar or newsletter? Communicate more effectively with a student-driven newspaper. Have your students establish a school paper with this engaging project.

Spotlight on: Informational writing

Driving question: How can we establish a school newspaper to keep students and families informed about school and community events?

Audience: Students and families

PROCESS

1. Discuss with your principal what they would like to see in a school newsletter. Work with them to set aside a time and meeting place for the school newsletter after it has been established by your class.

2. Bring in copies of newspapers to show your class. You can also share online newspapers.

3. Tell your students that your class is going to establish a school newspaper and publish the first issue. Have your principal or another member of administration come in to class and tell students what they'd like to see in the school newspaper.

4. Work together as a class to make a list of the tasks they will need to complete to establish the newspaper.

5. Split students into groups based on their interests and the tasks on the list. You will likely have similar groups to these: editing, photography, layout and graphic design, and other support. All students will write articles to submit for the first publication, so a group is not needed for writing.

7. As students begin to organize the beginning of the newspaper, have students research what types of articles are in a newspaper and how these articles are formatted. Compare these to student newspapers, which you can often get copies of from local high schools or online.

8. Have students list the types of articles they will need for the newspaper. They may include current school and community events, reviews, how-to articles, and opinion pieces.

9. Begin with having students write about current events in the school and their community. This is a great way to teach about and practice informational writing. They can write about an event they recently attended or write about an upcoming event. Have students work together to gather information for their articles. If students participate in extracurricular activities, allow them to write about events they participate in. Events like sports tournaments and dance recitals will be of interest to students and their families that otherwise wouldn't know that these events occur in the community.

10. Have students that are a part of the photography group take photos for the articles. If an event already happened, students can find photos that people took at the event and get their permission to use them.

11. Have students work in their interest groups to prepare the first issue of the newspaper. They will need to choose the articles to include, edit them, add photographs, design the layout, and do anything else that needs to be prepared for publication.

12. Publish the first issue in print or online.

13. Now that the newspaper is established, transition it so that other students can take over jobs and work on it before or after school.

Other Connections: Connect this project with your social studies standards on current events.

61 POETRY SLAM

A poetry slam isn't your traditional poetry reading. This competitive event will get your students excited about writing impactful pieces of poetry.

Spotlight on: Poetry

Driving question: How can I create a poem that will make my voice heard?

Audience: Classroom and community

PROCESS

1. Schedule your poetry slam event and decide on the theme. You can have your students help decide the theme, if you'd like. It should relate to a current issue or a positive message. Bullying is a common theme for school poetry slams. An example of a positive message theme could be "What I'm thankful for."

2. Search YouTube for videos of student poetry slams to introduce the idea to your students. Have students research the format and rules for poetry slams.

3. Discuss how you can use poetry to share a message. Introduce types of poetry and use this step to help students learn your specific poetry standards. Students can use any type of poetry they find best conveys their message, but they should keep in mind that there should be a natural rhythm when reading their poem aloud.

4. Have students begin writing first drafts of their poems. Encourage them to write what they see, hear, taste, touch, and smell when thinking about their topic. They want to paint a picture using descriptive language. Tell them that personal stories their audience can relate to do very well in poetry slam competitions.

5. Build in several opportunities for critique and revision as they write their rough drafts. Don't wait until they're finished with their rough draft to give feedback.

6. Once they've finished their rough drafts, have them take turns reading their poems to small groups of two or three other students.

7. Discuss the reaction of the audience. Tell students that they want their audience to react out loud in order to increase their score during the poetry slam. Have students add to or revise their poems to attempt to get their audience to react (e.g., laugh, clap, gasp, or cry).

8. Develop final drafts of poems. Have students begin to practice reading their pieces out loud, planning areas to speed up or slow down, whisper or shout, and use facial expressions and movements to engage their audience.

9. Throw your poetry slam! You can have an audience of parents, staff members, and other students. Select judges in the audience to give numerical scores for each poem.

10. Announce the winner and celebrate the hard work of your students. You may also choose to publish these poems in print or online.

Other Connections: Teach your students about figurative language during this project. Using figurative language is another great method of expression in poetry.

62 CANDY BAR MARKETING

Your students will be so excited when you bring in a pile of different candy bars to start this project! This PBL activity combines persuasive techniques with marketing skills and research in a well-rounded, competitive project. Note: If you have a student with a nut allergy, substitute candy bars with a non-food product.

Spotlight on: Persuasive writing

Driving question: How can we persuade kids to buy our candy bars over other candy bars?

Audience: Other students

PROCESS

1. Before beginning, find another teacher that would like to partner with you and your students. They can do the project as well, or they can just be participants when it comes time to choose the best persuasive pieces.

2. Arrange students in small groups of three. Bring in enough candy bars so that there is one bar for each group of three students. Randomly assign a candy bar to each group. I suggest finding a variety of candy bar types that most kids aren't familiar with, like the "classic" candy bars.

3. Discuss persuasive techniques. You can teach your students all eight persuasive techniques, or use just a few that you think your students will easily understand. Read a variety of persuasive writing pieces and make lists of what the authors do to convince you to agree with them. Watch commercials for candy bars and similar products and take notes on the persuasive techniques they use.

4. Have each group of students choose a few things they observed in the commercials or writing pieces that they want to incorporate in their own persuasive pieces. For example, if they notice repetition of the product name, they can easily choose to include that in their writing.

5. After your students decide what persuasive techniques they want to use in their writing, have them each work on one paragraph persuading someone to buy their candy bar. They can open the candy up and try it so they know what it tastes like, if they haven't devoured it already by this step. Have them keep the wrapper intact.

6. Next, have groups read and discuss each member's paragraph. Work with each group to choose the best points and techniques to combine into one perfect persuasive paragraph per group.

7. Once the paragraphs have been revised and edited, have groups write their final paragraphs on a large poster. Hang these posters around the room. Don't allow students to draw or decorate. The posters should only have their text on it.

8. Have the students in the other class come in to read the posters. Give each student in the visiting class a sticky note. Have them read each poster and select the one they think advertises the best candy bar by placing their sticky note on that poster.

9. After the visiting students return to their classroom, have your students reflect on their persuasive paragraphs. Analyze the one with the most sticky notes on it to determine why it was so popular. Discuss the power of text and how just a paragraph convinced students that it was the best candy bar.

Other Connections: After completing this project, students can continue exploring this topic by watching commercials and creating their own commercial for their candy bar. This ties into any verbal standards you may have, such as learning persuasive speech skills.

63 MEMOIRS

Memoirs are a great way to teach a multitude of both reading and writing standards, and there are many different types of memoirs that are perfect for grades 3 through 5. In this activity, your students will learn about someone else's history while writing about their own.

Spotlight on: Memoirs

Driving question: How can I write a short memoir to share with my family that incorporates some of the elements of the memoirs we are reading?

Audience: Family

PROCESS

1. Borrow as many kid-friendly memoirs as you can from your local library. You can read excerpts from longer books and even get bite-sized memoirs in the form of picture books. If you have access to a school library, have students search for memoirs they are interested in with the help of the librarian.

2. Read lots of examples together, individually, and in small groups, and make a list of common themes and elements of memoirs. Analyze the different formats of the memoirs.

3. Tell students that they will each be writing a short memoir around an important part of their life. It could incorporate a struggle they've had to deal with, a special tradition with a family member, or an important life event.

4. Have students brainstorm ideas for their memoir. Provide an opportunity for feedback, and have students use this feedback to choose the overall topic and theme for their memoir.

5. Begin writing memoirs. Allow students to choose how their memoirs will be formatted. By now, your class will have learned that memoirs come in many different shapes and sizes.

6. Continue to have students read and analyze different memoirs. Use excerpts from longer books, do read-alouds, and encourage students to read memoirs on their own time.

7. Model the writing process as students work on their memoirs. Build in a lot of time for critique and revision.

8. After students write their final drafts, have them format their memoirs into books. They've seen a lot of different formatting examples, so hopefully you will see a lot of very different memoir designs.

9. Have students share their memoirs with their families.

Other Connections: Incorporate technology into this project by creating an ebook using all of the student memoirs. This can be easily shared with all of the students and their families so that everyone can enjoy reading the different memoirs.

64 PARTY PLANNER

I thought of this project idea one year when it was the Monday before Valentine's Day and I had nothing ready for our class party. I enlisted the help of my students for that party, and they planned all of our class parties from then on!

Spotlight on: Reading comprehension and procedure writing

Driving question: How can we create something unique for a class party that students and family members will enjoy?

Audience: Students and family members

PROCESS

1. Gather materials that students can use for inspiration, such as magazines, books, and digital resources on holidays and planning parties. My favorite sources are magazines with recipes and decoration ideas that are relevant to the holiday. Ask parents to send in any relevant magazines that they've already read and are willing to donate. Have students use these materials to research what goes into planning a party.

2. As a class, brainstorm the items you will need for the party. Some examples are food, decorations, and games. List the items that need to be planned for and the order they will be taken care of. Your first order of business may be to make a list of everyone coming to the party.

3. Work on planning the party together as a class, but send students off to work in pairs and small groups for larger tasks like coming up with and creating decorations.

4. Have students take care of everything you normally do to plan a party. This includes making a list of what food is needed and making a sign-up sheet for bringing in different foods.

5. Encourage in-depth inquiry into topics that each individual student is interested in. They should be asking questions about planning parties, taking the initiative to answer these questions, and finding ways to help. Some students will be more interested in putting together a fun game, while others are crafty and will find a decoration on YouTube that they want to recreate. Make sure that every student has something unique they can create for the party.

6. Have each student analyze the steps they followed to complete their unique party piece and write out the procedure. Model what procedure writing looks like for students, using a craft, recipe, or game that you created for the party.

7. Have students each share what they made for the party and the process for making it.

8. Have students create final drafts of their procedures that include the materials, steps they took, and photos or drawings of their unique piece of the party.

9. Put all the final procedure pieces into one big party planning book to keep ideas for next year. Family members can also view the book and learn about what their student made when they attend the party!

Other Connections: Make a math connection by having students find the total cost of the materials for the game, recipe, or craft that they made. Add up the cost of every person's contribution to find the total cost of the party.

65 FOLKTALES AROUND THE WORLD

In this activity, your students will have to do in-depth inquiry into different folktales in order to become experts on them before they present the stories to younger students. All you need to begin is another teacher willing to let your students come read to their students (preschool through second grade).

Spotlight on: Folktales

Driving question: How can I introduce younger students to the magic of folktales?

Audience: Younger students

PROCESS

1. Tell your students which class you'll be working with. Get them excited about working with these kids by discussing some of their favorite reading lessons from that grade level.

2. Teach students what a folktale is. Provide students with a variety of different folktales to read. I like to bring in library books, printed stories, and video representations of folktales. Label each folktale by the area of the world it's from. Keep out a large world map for students so they can find the origin of each story.

3. After students have had ample time to read and explore folktales from around the world, have each student choose folktales from one culture to focus on for their projects. Group students into pairs based on this choice.

4. Have each pair further research the culture they chose. Have them find and read as many different folktales from this culture as they can.

5. As a class, make a list of common elements they see in these folktales. Conduct a whole group discussion on similar elements, using this discussion to further teach about the elements of a folktale.

6. Have each pair choose a folktale from the culture they researched that they think would be the most fun to read to the younger students. Have students practice reading this folktale aloud in a way that is fun and engaging for young kids.

7. Have students write down facts to share with the younger students to introduce them to this culture's folktales. They can even bring a small map to show the younger students where in the world this folktale originated. Students should also come up with questions to ask the younger children after reading.

8. Assign two to three students from the class you're partnering with to each of your student pairs. Have your students introduce the culture, read the folktale, and then ask the younger students their prepared questions. If you have time, have the younger students rotate through a few different folktales, so that your students get the opportunity to present their information several times.

Other Connections: Tie in geography standards by having each student keep an individual map of the world where they can label the different regions that the folktales each pair of students reads is from.

66 COLORFUL CALENDARS

We've created calendars in the past to raise money for our school, but I love this educational twist on the usual calendar-designing task. If you don't want to use this as a fundraiser, ignore the fundraising steps and make a few small changes to the driving question.

Spotlight on: Figurative language

Driving question: How can we use figurative language to create colorful calendars that people are willing to buy during our calendar fundraiser?

Audience: Parents and community members

PROCESS

1. Bring in your favorite wall calendar, or show students pictures of wall calendars online. Discuss how you can design calendars to sell and raise money for your school.

2. Tell students that one of the themes of your wall calendar is going to be figurative language. Give students a list of the types of figurative language you want them to learn more about. Create an organizer for them to record details and examples of each type of figurative language on your list. Provide them with a way to research and learn about each type. I sometimes do this by sharing a collection of videos for them to watch and take notes on.

3. After researching, have students discuss examples of each type of figurative language. Find exact quotes for each. Use these quotes as inspiration for designing the calendars.

4. Split students into groups of six. This will let each student in the group create two months of the calendar. Groups of 12 can also work if you want to shorten the project and only have a few variations of the calendar.

5. Assign a type of figurative language to each month. In grades 3 through 5, we usually focus on six to eight different types of figurative language. You will have to repeat many of them for a second month.

6. Have students use the quotes they gathered earlier as inspiration for drawings. They should match the figurative language in the quotes to the different months. Have them write the quotes under their drawings on the calendar pages.

7. Facilitate while they make their designs. Have them do their final designs on cardstock if you'll be auctioning off the originals. Otherwise, have them design on regular paper that you can copy onto cardstock later. If your students have devices, you can easily integrate technology by having them design the calendar pages digitally.

8. Print blank calendars and add the designs. Keep a copy of each calendar page to display on the wall, showing the example of figurative language.

9. Sell copies of the calendars or auction off the original copies.

Other Connections: Incorporate poetry into this activity by having students write short poems for each page that incorporates the figurative language. Have them illustrate to match the poems.

67 GAME NIGHT

Many schools put on family game nights every month to get to know the families of their students better, creating a positive connection between school and home. Use this project to have your students help you plan a family game night based on a chapter book they're reading.

Spotlight on: Reading comprehension and informational writing

Driving question: How can we create a board game for family game night that goes with the theme of our book?

Audience: Students and family

PROCESS

1. Plan the game night far enough in the future to allow students to complete their books.

2. Have students read their chosen books in small groups, based off the book choice they're most interested in. I usually run this like a book club, where students group themselves based on their favorite book genre and then go to the school library to find a book they want to read together.

3. Switch from reading books to researching board games. Have them make a list of some of the most popular board games, noting what made them popular.

4. Have them brainstorm ideas for a game that will match the theme of their book. They can continue to research board games, focusing on games that are themed around books or movies.

5. As they read, have them take notes on different elements of literature, like characters, plot, figurative language, and theme.

Facilitate discussions of these elements to help students apply their knowledge of the elements of literature.

6. Help students continue to research and discuss board game ideas until they come up with the procedure for their game. If your students are struggling with this step, it's a good idea to bring in a few games for them to play. This will help them see the elements of gameplay and what a game box includes (e.g., game board, instructions, and player pieces).

7. Have students create their board games. In this step, they should be working on the game board. After they finish the game board, they should practice playing and get feedback before writing the instructions. I suggest students get feedback from a few different partners before finalizing the game boards.

8. Share game instructions from several games with students, so that they can determine what needs to go in their game's instructions.

9. Have students finish their game board and instructions.

10. Debut the games for families at family game night!

Other Connections: I hinted in Step 5 that you can incorporate standards relating to literature. Determine what you want students to focus on when reading their novels, and create generic student organizers that have them look for that focus in their different books. You can have students help you make these organizers as well. If you want to cover something that students haven't learned yet, like figurative language, you can throw in a mini-lesson and have students search for figurative language in their novels.

68 INTERNET SAFETY

Internet safety instruction can be a bit dull. Make this important information more exciting by having your students build their own curriculum!

Spotlight on: Research and informational writing

Driving question: How can we create lessons to teach kids how to safely use the internet?

Audience: Kids using the internet

PROCESS

1. Collect reading materials, videos, and infographics that give students the information they need about internet safety.

2. Lead a discussion with students about what they know to stay safe online. Chances are, your students already know a little bit about internet safety. Make a list of what they already know.

3. Ask students what they don't know about internet safety. Record all their questions.

4. Tell students that they will be making an internet safety lesson for other kids. Split students up into groups that focus on the different areas of internet safety, such as personal information/privacy, talking safely, cyber bullying, and credible sources (what websites can we trust?). You can brainstorm additional areas with your students, as well.

5. Have each group brainstorm some ideas based on what they already know about the topic, then return to the list of things they didn't know and research any questions on the list that relate to their area.

6. Let students decide how they want to teach other kids about their topics. Even with limited technology, they can make videos, digital presentations, and digital worksheets. You can store each item as a module on a website you and your class create on internet safety. You can also put together media and create an assembly for the students at your school.

7. Have the groups put together their lessons. Once they've received feedback and are polished, publish or present these lessons.

Other Connections: A fantastic opinion writing prompt goes very well with this project: Should kids have cell phones? Another option is: At what age should a kid have a cell phone?

69 MOVIE ADAPTATION

Nothing is more exciting than finding out a book you love is being turned into a movie! This project is a great way to merge book clubs and PBL by having students create a movie adaptation for the book they're reading.

Spotlight on: Reading comprehension

Driving question: How can we turn a book into a movie that the author would approve of?

Audience: Author

PROCESS

1. Most authors are very excited to hear about students reading their books. After your book clubs choose their books, contact all of the authors to let them know what your students will be doing. You don't need the author to respond or be involved in the project, but sometimes they do send a response, and that is very exciting!

2. Run your book clubs the way you normally would. As your students are reading, they should discuss and take notes on the events they want to include in the movie adaptation.

3. About halfway through reading the books, have students research the author. Discuss how an author will often have a vision for how their book should be made into a movie. This vision is important, and learning more about the author can help students come up with ideas for an adaptation that the author would approve of.

4. Students should continue to brainstorm and discuss ideas as they read. Have students put sticky notes on pages with really important events that they know need to be in the movie.

5. When they finish their books, it's time for them to start planning their adaptations. They can choose how they want to present it, but a storyboard would be a simple way to show the main events. They can also include drawings of what the characters would look like, include suggestions for actors that would play the characters, and create a movie poster.

6. After they've completely outlined the movie and it's ready to be presented to the author, put it all in a folder in preparation to submit it to the author. My students did one years ago for Lois Lowry that said "For Lois Lowry's Eyes Only" and had "top secret" stamped on it. I loved their creativity!

7. Have them make a video of their group presenting the materials to the author. Send the video and any print materials like storyboards and movie posters to the author with a note explaining what your class did with their book. If you can't find an email address for the author, email these items to their publisher. They're usually happy to pass them on.

Other Connections: After this project, read a book that actually has a movie adaptation. This will keep students very engaged in the reading as they imagine how it was adapted into a movie. Watch the movie together and discuss the adaptation in relation to how they did their adaptations.

70 SPELLING BEE

Spelling can be a somewhat boring aspect of school, and most of the time it's naturally incorporated into our ELA-based projects. However, this project gives you the opportunity to get students involved in a school event that usually only a handful of kids end up involved in. Incorporate your regular spelling lessons and quizzes into this project.

Spotlight on: Spelling

Driving question: How can we put on a school spelling bee that will be fun for students?

Audience: Students

PROCESS

1. As a class, watch videos of school spelling bees. Have students read the rules for spelling bees. Let them know that they have to follow these rules, but that they can add more elements of fun to the event.

2. Have students make a list of everything they need to plan in order to put on a spelling bee. These will be things like the location, word lists, judges, and competitors.

3. Work as a class to research what other schools do for each of the things on the list. Where do most schools hold their spelling bees? Where can you hold yours? How can you make the space more fun? It wouldn't be surprising to hear students come up with the idea of decorating the auditorium with bees for the spelling bee!

4. Plan the event together. Have students act out how their spelling bee will go by memorizing word lists and participating in mock spelling bees.

5. Have students split off into small groups to complete the final tasks for the spelling bee. Have them provide other classrooms with word lists and directions on how to choose a class representative to compete in the bee.

6. Put on the event. Afterward, have students reflect on what they learned about spelling and spelling bees during this project.

Other Connections: If you're still explicitly teaching spelling words, run a mock spelling bee to practice for future spelling quizzes. I prefer to incorporate most of my spelling practice into writing instruction, but I continue to relate it to the spelling bee project by having students look a word up in the dictionary and spell it aloud for me. They really see the importance of spelling after putting on this event where spelling is the focus!

71 **LOCAL LEADER**

Local projects are so meaningful to students. In this activity, your students will honor local leaders while learning about what it means to be a leader in the community.

> **Spotlight on:** Descriptive writing
>
> **Driving question:** How can I honor a local leader that makes a difference in our community?
>
> **Audience:** Community

PROCESS

1. Have your students make a list of adults they know in the community that are important leaders. This could be sports team coaches, the mayor, principals, one of their parents, etc.

2. Contact these leaders. Have several come into the class to talk about what it means to be a leader. Facilitate while students further research what it means to be a leader. They can do this by reading books and articles about famous leaders from the past.

3. Have students work in small groups to create a project that honors each leader. They can choose the leader that they admire the most after listening to them speak to the class.

4. Have students write questions to ask each leader, then submit those questions to be answered.

5. Discuss descriptive writing. How can they describe each leader and what they do for the community? Have students write descriptive pieces about their chosen leaders.

6. Have each group decide how they will honor the leaders. Tell them that they must use their descriptive writing to guide their end product. Some end products may be a song or rap, an award with text describing what the leader has done for the community, or a small statue showing them doing what they do best.

7. Complete the projects. Invite these leaders back in to honor them.

Other Connections: You can make several connections to social studies in this project. One of my favorite books to lead this project is *Who Was Martin Luther King, Jr.?* by Bonnie Bader.

72 BE THE CHANGE

During this very important project, your students will work to create an anti-bullying campaign. They will learn persuasive techniques to convince other students to get involved in standing up to bullies.

Spotlight on: Persuasive techniques

Driving question: How can our class create an anti-bullying campaign that makes our school a safer place?

Audience: Students

PROCESS

1. Discuss bullying as a class. Have students share some of the instances they've seen of bullying in the past (without mentioning names).

2. Discuss what works and what doesn't with anti-bullying campaigns. Talk a little about how if kids can't connect to a campaign or aren't persuaded properly, they won't take action. Teach them about persuasive techniques as a part of this discussion.

3. Have students work in pairs to research all eight persuasive techniques, or just a few that are appropriate for your grade level. View a variety of anti-bullying campaigns from the last 10 years and make lists of what they do to convince you to agree with them. Discuss which ones are effective, and which aren't.

4. Make a list of types of bullying (e.g., cyber, physical, verbal, and social). Split students into groups that will address each type of bullying.

5. Have each group research ways to stop their type of bullying. Have them discuss what they think would work best for your school.

6. After they've decided how to tackle the issues, have each group create a plan for how they will present this solution to the students in your school. Have them incorporate what they learned about persuasive techniques to persuade students to take the actions being recommended.

7. Allow students to decide which method they'll use to deliver this information. They can make videos, games, worksheets, etc. Allow them plenty of time to create their materials.

8. Put all the materials together to make an anti-bullying "course." The best way to share this would be on a school website where students can go through each module, in class or at home.

Other Connections: Use the opinion-writing prompt: Should bullies be arrested? There was a great article about this on Newsela (www.newsela.com) that really got my students thinking. They were very split on the issue, which means it's a great topic to have students write about!

73 COLLEGE APPLICATION

The Saving for College project (page 139) in the math section of this book has students budget for college. This PBL activity would be a great companion if you're looking to connect ELA and math.

Spotlight on: Persuasive writing

Driving question: How can I write a college application letter that convinces my dream college to accept me?

Audience: College advisor

PROCESS

1. Discuss colleges and careers. If you can, have someone come from a local college to tell you about the type of students they're looking for when they review applications. A bonus is that they will definitely discuss good grades, which will help students see the importance of working hard to get good grades.

2. Have students discuss careers they would like to have. Have them research what colleges have the best programs for each career. This is very similar to the process in Saving for College, and you can definitely do both of these concurrently.

3. Discuss college applications. Show students some examples of what applications look like, and discuss application letters.

4. Have students work in small groups to make lists of what college advisors are looking for when they review applications. Have them use the information from the college advisor that visited, and ask them to research the admissions requirements at a college they're interested in for their career option. Fifth graders will have no trouble doing this, but fourth graders will need a lot more scaffolding. Third graders will need to complete this part of the project as a class.

5. Have each student brainstorm some reasons why they are a great student. Have them keep in mind what their chosen college is looking for in a student.

6. Model formatting for writing a persuasive letter.

7. Have students write persuasive letters to the colleges, explaining why the college should accept them as students once they graduate. To add to the experience, have students choose some work samples from class to attach to their letters. These samples should show the exemplary work that they do as students in your class.

8. "Send" the applications off. Stamp them with an "Accepted" stamp and return them to your students. Have them reflect on the process, discussing how this will help them in the future with their actual college applications.

Other Connections: In addition to the math connection mentioned above, you can bring in a ton of reading passages about the different careers the class has chosen. Check out books from the library about different colleges, states they can visit, and careers.

74 LET'S PUBLISH! (DIGITAL)

I love publishing student writing. This project-based learning activity gives students the tools they need to write and publish a digital magazine that focuses on creative writing.

Spotlight on: Creative writing

Driving question: How can we publish our creative writing pieces as a part of a digital magazine?

Audience: Online magazine readers

PROCESS

1. Share some online publications with your students. Tell them that they will be creating their own digital magazine using creative writing pieces. Have them work together to research different digital magazines and make a list of what they include that make people purchase them. Scholastic News (sn3.scholastic.com) has a great digital magazine, and they usually offer a one-month sample on their website that your students can use.

2. Talk about copyright and fair use when you discuss what information and images they can share. Bring in information about internet safety. Create pen names to use online for sharing pieces they've authored.

3. Create a name for your class' digital magazine.

4. Teach the elements of creative writing. Have students begin to brainstorm for their first writing pieces.

5. Have students help you set up the digital magazine. You can use any platform you choose, but Zinepal (www.zinepal.com) is a very popular one. I've also used Google Slides with the slide size changed to 8.5 x 11, merged all student slides, then converted it to one PDF document.

6. Have your artistic students create the title and layout design for the magazine. Have them make a page template that they can share with all students.

7. Have students continue writing creative pieces. When the pieces are polished and ready to publish, have students add them to the template.

8. Put all the writing pieces together in one document. Add the finishing touches and publish the digital magazine. You can add it to your school's website, or share in any other way.

Other Connections: Have students share other writing pieces to their digital magazine. This can be used with any writing type that they create in the future, like poems and opinion pieces.

75 LET'S PUBLISH! (PRINT)

If you don't have access to a lot of technology, this project is another great option for publishing student pieces. Find a local business that will distribute the publications so your magazine reaches more people.

Spotlight on: Creative writing

Driving question: How can we publish our creative writing pieces as a part of a print magazine?

Audience: Families and community members

PROCESS

1. Before beginning, make some contacts in the community that would be willing to display a few copies (that you provide) of your print magazine. Places like local art co-ops and city offices are usually happy to display student work.

2. Share several print magazines with your students. Magazines that share creative writing pieces are the best. Tell them that they will be creating their own print magazine using creative writing pieces. Have them make a list of the types of pieces included in these magazines.

3. Talk about copyright and fair use when you discuss what information and images they can share in their print magazines. Create pen names to use for sharing pieces they've authored if you're sharing publicly.

4. Create a name for your class' print magazine.

5. Teach the elements of creative writing. Have students begin to brainstorm for their first writing pieces.

6. Have students help you set up the print magazine. Ask your artistic students to create the title and layout design for the magazine. Have them make a page template that they can share with all students, then make copies. Have them also make a cover design for the front page of the magazine.

7. Continue writing creative pieces. When the pieces are polished and ready to publish, have students add them to the template.

8. Make copies and place the cover on front. Publish by making copies for each student, as well as some copies for your front office and any location that has agreed to display the magazine.

Other Connections: Just like with the digital magazine, you can reuse your templates to publish any of your students' work. It would be great to publish an edition of your print magazine every month, showcasing any style of writing that your students learned to write.

CHAPTER 6

SOCIAL STUDIES

76 CREATE A BILL

Want to bring this process to life for your students? Have students participate in the process of creating a bill and following it until it becomes a law!

Spotlight on: American government

Driving question: How can I create a bill that helps people and help it become a law?

Audience: Congressperson, students

PROCESS

1. Contact a local congressperson using the representative finder on the House of Representatives' website. Ask them to help or provide the information of someone who can help with this project. Some are happy to get involved, while others may have a staff member or intern represent them.

2. Have students research the process of a bill becoming a law. Make a graphic representation of the process as a class.

3. Provide students with information so that they can research a few of the bills that recently became law.

4. Have students come up with a list of laws that would make our country better, but aren't already in effect. Have students ask their families what would make their lives better. Research this list and narrow it down to the best ideas.

5. Have students split into groups based on which of these laws they're most passionate about.

6. Facilitate while each student creates a presentation to introduce the bill.

7. When ready, have students "send the bill to committee" for research and revision. You can do this by having two groups work together to improve both of their bills.

8. Next, form a House and a Senate. Have each group bring their bill to either the House or the Senate. Have them debate it and make any changes, then vote. If it passes the House, repeat the process in the Senate.

9. Bills that make it through both the House and the Senate will go to the President last. This can be you or a student you appoint. The president can veto or let it pass.

Other Connections: Tie in persuasive writing by having students submit a written introduction to the bill that explains its importance.

77 SCHOOL MAP

Show students the importance of map skills by helping create maps for your school to give to new students and visitors. This is also a great way to get to know the different areas of your school.

Spotlight on: Map skills

Driving question: How can we create a map that will help new students and visitors locate important areas of the school?

Audience: New students and school visitors

PROCESS

1. Introduce this project by showing students a current map of the school, if you have one. Tell students that they are going to work in groups to create a map of the school for new students and visitors.

2. Introduce students to the vocabulary you want them to use when creating their maps. Have them take notes on each word. Some important vocabulary words you may want to include are scale, legend, compass, cardinal directions (north, south, east, west), and intermediate directions (NE, SE, NW, SW).

3. Break students off into groups of three.

4. Model how to set up maps on graph paper. Show students which way faces north. Assist students in drawing the outline of the building and labeling each wall and the way it faces.

5. Have each student bring graph paper, pencil, and a clipboard as you tour the school. Stop in each location and outline the area on the map.

6. Return to the classroom. Have groups work together to share their maps and get feedback. Have the students in each group work together to create a single group map that accurately shows the layout of the school and incorporates any creative ideas students have for the maps. Discuss scale further and estimate the size of each room on the map. Use critical thinking skills to make sure that the maps make sense. For example, if your classroom is shown as larger than the cafeteria on the map, did they do a good job estimating the size of the cafeteria?

7. Work to revise until each group has their best map.

8. Have each group decide what they want their map to be used for. From this decision, they will each create a different end product. Some possible end products are a large map to display in the cafeteria showing the path from the cafeteria to the bathrooms (if they're in a separate location), a digital map that visitors and new students can get by scanning a QR code with their device, or small handheld maps for new students to tape in their planners. Their ideas should reflect the needs of your individual school.

9. Have students present their end products to administrators in your building, and put them into action so that new students and visitors have these great resources!

Other Connections: You can easily extend this project by continuing with a unit on maps of states and countries. This will also extend the map vocabulary used to include terms like latitude and longitude.

78 PRESENT-DAY EXPLORERS

This project makes history relevant by tying in past explorers with present-day exploration.

Spotlight on: Early explorers and geography

Driving question: How can we use what we learn about past exploration to create a virtual trip to a place that students in our class have never explored?

Audience: Self

PROCESS

1. Begin by introducing students to early explorers (e.g., Christopher Columbus, Francisco Vázquez de Coronado). Read about these explorers. Discuss their goals, obstacles, and accomplishments. Reflect on why they risked their lives to explore the unexplored.

2. Work as a class to make a list of all the technological developments that made sea exploration by latitude and longitude possible (e.g., compass, sextant, astrolabe, seaworthy ships, chronometers, gunpowder). Have students explore each of these items to learn more about what they did and what they helped early explorers accomplish.

3. As a class, make a list of today's technological tools that help us explore new areas and share information with people back home (e.g., cameras, phones, GPS, planes).

4. Trace the routes of some of the early explorers. Tie in map skills during this part of the project.

5. Bring the project back to present day by having students each come up with an area of the world they want to explore. They should choose places that are exotic to them, preferably a place on a different continent.

6. Group students together based on the locations they choose. Have each group narrow down their exploration route. Refer to the routes of the early explorers to see how they can possibly connect one location to the next. Have students use a blank world map to map out their journeys from where they live to the places they will be exploring.

7. Have each group make a list of goals and obstacles for their exploration. Refer to the goals and obstacles of the early explorers. Discuss how goals and obstacles of exploration are different in the modern day.

8. Once students finalize their exploration routes, have them begin working together to explore the routes virtually. Have them find photos, videos, and written text about each area.

9. Each group should use all these resources to create a virtual tour for the class. Allow them to choose how they will present their virtual tours. There are a lot of great multimedia programs they can use if they have access to technology.

10. Within their presentation, students should explain their modern-day goals, obstacles, and accomplishments while exploring this area.

Other Connections: Merge this project and the Travel Abroad project (page 109) in the math section of this book to hit social studies, math, and ELA standards in one.

79 THE OREGON TRAIL

In this project, students will make a strategic plan to move their family west, addressing the challenges and risks that pioneers faced.

Spotlight on: Pioneers

Driving question: How can I prepare my family to travel west on the Oregon Trail?

Audience: Family

PROCESS

1. Introduce the project using the picture book *Roughing It on the Oregon Trail* by Diane Stanley. I've found that this fictional story about a time-traveling grandma who takes her twin grandkids back to the time period we are studying is a fun way to explain what we're doing in this scenario.

2. Have students inquire into why families decided to take this journey on the Oregon Trail. Have each student make a pro/con list as if they were deciding to move their own families west.

3. Explore a map of the Oregon Trail. Print a map of the US, or have them use their devices to create their own map of where their family will travel on the Oregon Trail. Use physical maps of the US to identify parts of the journey that will be difficult (e.g., crossing rivers and mountains).

4. Set up resources for your students to explore the tools and technologies that pioneers brought to help them survive during the trip and after settling on new land. They will each do research for their own individual families, but can work in small groups to discuss their research.

5. Research wagons. Have students answer questions important to their journey, such as "How large were the wagons, and how much weight would they hold?"

6. Have the class begin to design wagons. Have each student sketch out their wagon's layout and draw where each item they want to bring will go. Have them begin with food and water, then branch out into other helpful items.

7. Further explore the risks and challenges of the journey. Students will need to revise wagon contents to reflect any new items that they will need to pack for their family.

8. Have each student create a plan for their family, listing what each individual family member will need to bring on the journey and what the journey will be like.

9. Arrange all your wagons in a class caravan. Create a large poster showing each family's spot in the long line of wagons traveling west together.

Other Connections: Connect social studies and writing by having students pretend to take the Oregon Trail route with their families. Have them keep a journal of their travels. You can also take the lesson one step further by having them design their settlements, researching homes of that era.

80 MUSEUM EXHIBIT: CIVIL WAR TECHNOLOGY

Your students will discover how cool social studies really is as they explore the technology used during the Civil War. From communication to weaponry, there's something for every student in this project!

> **Spotlight on:** Civil War
>
> **Driving question:** How can we create a museum exhibit that will teach other kids about the Civil War?
>
> **Audience:** Other students

PROCESS

1. Before beginning, find a space suitable for the student exhibits. Try to contact someone from a local museum willing to do some community outreach by coming to your classroom to talk about the process of preparing a new exhibit. It's also a great idea to find a local history professor, or a hobbyist interested in the Civil War, that will come talk to your class.

2. Introduce the Civil War to students. Have them explore timelines and maps to get an idea of where and when the Civil War took place. Discuss the reasons for the Civil War.

3. Tell students that they will be creating exhibits for kids interested in the Civil War. Have students fill out an interest survey to find out what aspects of the Civil War they would be most interested in. Some examples are weapons, medicine, communication, and transportation. Group students into small groups based on their interest surveys.

4. Have each group explore the topic that they're interested in. For example, one group may explore hydrogen-filled passenger balloons and submarines as a part of their research on Civil War transportation technology.

5. Facilitate while students continue to inquire about and discuss their topics.

6. Have each group create a plan for their exhibit. It should include multiple pieces such as models, written explanations, and visuals like historical photographs, maps, and timelines.

7. Allow each group plenty of time to create their exhibits. Have students write down some facts that they can present to people who visit the exhibits.

8. Prepare the exhibits to be displayed. Ask for parent volunteers to help with this part of the project, and invite families and other kids to see the end product.

Other Connections: Discuss the importance of inventors and engineers during this time period. Make a connection to science by looking at how one or more of these pieces of technology was engineered.

81 BUILD A STATUE

Although this project idea can be easily modified for any social studies concept, I really enjoy using it with the topic of the American Revolution. Your students will love bringing out their artistic sides when they create their very own statues.

Spotlight on: The American Revolution

Driving question: How can we design a statue that depicts an important battle from the American Revolution?

Audience: Residents of areas near battle sites

1. Before beginning, make a list of the specific battles during the American Revolution that you or your standards deem necessary to teach. Get together with your art teacher (if you have one), to devise a plan for creating the sculptures. If you have limited resources, it's totally fine to have them make the statues out of play dough.

2. Provide students with resources so that they can read a summary of each battle. Have them choose the battle they're most interested in, then arrange students in groups of three or four based on their interests. If you don't have enough battles on your list for groups that small, it's OK to allow two groups to create a statue for the same battle.

3. In groups, have students further research their battles. Provide them with an organizer so they can individually take notes.

4. Have each group work together to design their statue. Have them draw it from the front, back, and side views. Allow them to choose what part of the battle the statue will represent. It could be a depiction of the battle, a famous person they want to honor, or an icon representing the battle.

5. Have students find a present-day town that this battle took place in or near. This is the town that they will be planning the statue for. If you can, make connections with people in each town to have students send their statue ideas to. Alternatively, you can organize all their ideas on a website that people can search.

6. Provide students with supplies for creating the statues. Determine what each person in each group will do for the statue before beginning. Each student should create one part of the statue. Students that aren't as artistic can stand and act out the statue as a model for another student that is molding a person, or they can work on accessories or small accent pieces. Give students plenty of time to create the statues.

7. When everyone is finished, submit the statue ideas to the towns or website. Take photos of each statue and create a large class map with the statue photos over the location of each battle. Have students write the dates of their battles on the map.

Other Connections: Have students practice measurement by making their own supplies. They can make play dough with just salt, flour, and water, or something more complex like sculpting clay. You can also incorporate a variety of art standards into this project.

82 MUSEUM EXHIBIT: LIFE IN ANCIENT ROME

The aspects of life in ancient Rome have always intrigued me, which is why this was the first social studies project-based learning activity I did with my students.

Spotlight on: Ancient Rome

Driving question: How can I recreate a piece of life in ancient Rome for a museum exhibit?

Audience: Other students

PROCESS

1. Send home letters telling parents about the project and letting them know that students may want to use materials from home. My students brought cardboard, clay, fabric, jewelry-making supplies, and more. I provided paint, paintbrushes, a hot glue gun (under strict supervision), and a few other small supplies that students requested.

2. Create a station for each part of life in ancient Rome: government, military, architecture, and everyday life (dress, music, and food will fit into this category). Place a short article about that facet of life at each station. Have students rotate through, taking notes and discussing the pieces that they're interested in. At the end of this activity, each student should have an idea of what they're most interested in.

3. Have students join the group that matches their interests. Within their groups, each student will create their own "piece of life in ancient Rome." Give them ample time to research about their topics, so they can choose from more than what was in the small articles you provided.

4. Have each student submit a project plan. The better their inquiry, the greater variety of projects you will have. Within my architecture group, I had students creating several buildings, aqueducts, and obelisks. My everyday life group had an even bigger variety, with students working on ancient Roman jewelry, coins, and even musical instruments.

5. Gather materials and continue research. Each student should be an expert on what they are creating. They should know how it works, and not just be copying a design from an image.

6. Give students time to work on their items. After they have revised and made their projects the best that they can be, have them each create a museum "wall plaque" that explains their piece of life in ancient Rome.

7. Place all projects together in your exhibit. Have students come by to see the exhibits. Make sure all the wall plaques are hung so that students can read about pieces as they walk past, much like in a museum.

8. You can also have students work together to create a booklet for visitors that summarizes each project in their exhibit. This booklet can be on paper, or accessed with devices using a QR code.

Other Connections: I connected this project with our informational writing unit by having my students each write an informational essay on what they chose to create from life in ancient Rome. You can create a book with all of their essays that they can check out of your classroom library. My students were constantly borrowing that book to learn more about ancient Rome from their classmates!

83 DESIGN THE NEXT $20 BILL

After this project is completed, your students will have some definite opinions on which historical figure should be on the next $20 bill! I've used this project in the past with female historical figures, but it can be used with any list of historical figures that you want your students to study.

Spotlight on: Historical figures

Driving question: How can I choose a worthy person to honor when I design the next $20 bill?

Audience: Secretary of Treasury

PROCESS

1. Before beginning, decide which historical figures you want your students to focus on. You can leave it open-ended, so that they can choose any person, or you can provide a list for them to choose from if you have specific people that your standards want your students to learn about. For simplicity's sake, the steps below assume you provide them with a list of historical figures to choose from based on specific standards from a certain time period. There are many news articles out there about different historical figures being discussed for printing on future bills.

2. Have each student research the historical figures and write a short summary of each person's accomplishments.

3. Have students split into smaller groups based on the historical figure they believe is most worthy to be honored on our next $20 bill. They will each individually design their $20 bills, but these groups will allow them to collaborate while further inquiring about this person.

4. Once students have gathered evidence for why their person should be on the next $20 bill, have them begin designing the bill. Have them choose a photo of the person that they think will best fit in the proper place on the bill. Provide them with a blank $20 bill template and have them draw the person's face from the photo they chose.

5. Have students research who makes the decision on the design of the $20 bills. They will find that this is the Secretary of the Treasury.

6. Have students write a persuasive letter to the Secretary of the Treasury, explaining why the person they chose should be featured on the next $20 bill. Have them include their designs. Make copies of these and send them to the Secretary of the Treasury. The address can be found on the US Department of the Treasury's website (www.treasury.gov).

Other Connections: Have students debate their choices in class. This is a great way to tie in any speech and public speaking standards, while students learn more about all of the historical figures.

84 STATE FLAGS

This project requires additional equipment and adult help, but the home economics component is very much worth it!

Spotlight on: The 50 states

Driving question: How can we sew state flags for our school's state flag display?

Audience: Students and staff

PROCESS

1. Before beginning, get together a list of every parent and staff member you can find that enjoys sewing and is willing to help with this project. If the sewing element just doesn't work for your classroom, you can tweak the project to create the flags without the sewing component.

2. Determine where you want the flags to hang. They can be displayed in a hall or common area in the school. You'll need a place with a lot of wall room.

3. Depending on your class size, students will need to make two or three flags each in order to represent every state. The easiest way to assign flags is to have students come up one at a time to choose one state flag that they will research and create. The students that go last should be the first to choose their second (and third, if necessary) flags.

4. As a class, come up with an efficient organizer or note-taking page to organize the information you find during research. Together, make a list of questions students will be answering about their flags. Questions on the list should be related to the history of the flag's design.

5. Have students research their flags, using the organizer and question list to look for key details about their flags.

6. From their notes and research, have students write an essay about the history of their flags. Connect this project with informational writing by helping students organize their essay with an introduction, body paragraphs, and conclusion.

7. Have students write a detailed plan that includes the fabric colors, sizes, and steps they will do to sew their flags. Once they've completed their plans, they can begin to draw shapes on the fabric. Any detailed designs, like an animal, can be printed and traced onto the fabric.

8. Bring in your parent and staff volunteers to help students either hand sew or use sewing machines to sew the flags. This is my favorite part of the project! Alternatively, have students create flags using construction paper, or buy white stick flags for them to design using markers.

9. Display the flags in the order that the states were admitted to the union. Have students create small "plaques" that give a few points of information about the history behind their flag. Display these plaques under the flags for students to read.

Other Connections: Incorporate more literacy into this project by having students visit the library to check out books about their states. You can also teach students about the US flag using the picture book *The Flag We Love* by Pam Muñoz Ryan.

85 POSTCARD EXCHANGE

In this activity, your students will have the opportunity to work with students in other states during a fun postcard exchange! The easiest way to set up a postcard exchange like this is through a teacher Facebook group, but you could also find and contact schools in each state.

Spotlight on: The 50 states

Driving question: How can I create a postcard that will teach kids in other states about our wonderful state?

Audience: Kids in other states

PROCESS

1. Before beginning, connect with teachers in each state that are willing to participate. The best way to do this is by creating a Google Doc listing each state. Next to each state, have the participating teacher put in their name, email, and school's address. All you need is that information and a set date to send the postcards out by, and you're ready to go!

2. Show your students the Google Doc and discuss with them how the project is set up. As a class, create a short video giving the other classes directions on how to complete the postcard exchange. The video should have clear steps (e.g., Step 1: Learn about your state's history. Step 2: Design postcards about your state. Step 3: Address and mail your postcards to classrooms in each state. Step 4: Collect the postcards you get from other states to learn more about those states.).

3. After you've signed up a teacher from each state and set a due date, have your students start researching your state. Work as a class to make a list of what should be on each postcard. I suggest buying blank postcards for this project, but you can easily use thick paper to create the postcards. You can often find 50 blank postcards for under $10 on Amazon.

4. Have your students complete their research to create 50 postcards with images that represent your state and the two or three most important facts about the state's history. Each student will need to create two or three postcards, depending on the size of your class. Your students can use the same design on multiple postcards.

5. Assign each student a state for each postcard, then have them address the cards and add postage. Mail the postcards. If your students have email accounts, have them email the teachers from other schools letting them know that the postcards have been sent and your class can't wait to get responses! If your students don't have email accounts, you can send out a notice to all of the teachers.

6. As postcards come in, have students read them and keep track of the facts about each state. You can even make copies of each postcard for students to keep in their binders. As a class, come up with a fun way to display the postcards (e.g., on a giant map of the US) and share what you've learned about each state.

7. If something happens and you're missing a state, students can research and create a postcard for that state to finalize the project.

Other Connections: Learn the interesting history behind the US Postal Service by researching how it got started and how it's evolved since.

86 ARTIFACT DIG

This is a great way for your students to become experts on a topic by creating a hands-on activity for younger students to explore.

Spotlight on: Ancient civilizations

Driving question: How can we create a hands-on lesson to teach younger students about an ancient civilization?

Audience: Younger students

PROCESS

1. Find a teacher with younger students (preschool through second grade) to partner with for this project. There will be a literacy component that will benefit their students, as well as a hands-on artifact dig that their students will love, and they don't have to plan!

2. Tell your students that you will be creating a hands-on lesson for the other class. Mention the age of the students in the other class, and have your students share the type of lessons they learned best from at that age. They should come to the conclusion that picture books, songs, and hands-on activities are the best for teaching this age.

3. If your goal is to study a variety of ancient civilizations, provide reading materials your students can read about each one and form groups based on which they are most interested in. You can also choose one specific topic (e.g., ancient Egypt), and form mixed-ability groups of three to four students.

4. Have each group make a list of questions about their topic. Have them further inquire into these questions by doing additional research using selected websites, print material, or both.

5. After groups have had ample time to research and answer their questions on the topic, have them discuss the aspects of the civilizations that the younger kids will be most interested in learning about.

6. Have each group choose a picture book about the ancient civilization to begin their lessons. You can check out a variety of picture books on the topic from your local library, or work closely with your school librarian to have books available for your students to choose from. In the past, I've worked with our school librarian to set up a Donor's Choose project (www.donorschoose .org) for books on this and other topics we were studying that year, so that students will learn how to visit the library for resources.

7. Each group will use their picture book and research notes to create a fun, age-appropriate activity for the younger students: an artifact dig. Have students make a list of "artifacts" they can bring in for their dig. In the past, students have brought everything from small dolls wrapped in cloth to coins they made from clay for an ancient Egypt dig.

8. Make a plan for how you will complete your dig. If you have a sandbox, this can easily be used for the artifact dig. If not, use large storage tubs for the artifact dig and fill them with sand or dirt. Have students bring in supplies that the younger students will use to dig out the artifacts.

9. Have each group finalize their lessons. Have them summarize what they will do with the students, from reading the picture book to introducing the topic to completing the artifact dig. Students will need to create age-appropriate organizers for the younger students to keep track of the artifacts they find and the facts they learned about the ancient civilization. This could be as simple as having pictures of the artifacts on a page for kindergartners to circle as they find and learn about the artifact.

10. Pair each group of your students with a group of similar size from the class you're working with. Have your students read the picture book and tell the students about the artifact dig they'll be doing. Your students should provide all directions and supplies before beginning the dig. While the younger students dig, your students should be there to help them find artifacts. When artifacts are found, your students should explain what the artifacts are, using examples from the book that they read them.

11. Have the younger students give feedback to your students about the lesson. Ask them what they learned about the topic, and what their favorite part was.

Other Connections: Discuss what an archaeologist does and what tools they use at a real dig site. Read articles about recent discoveries in archaeology. You can find several student-friendly articles for free on Newsela.

87 ULTIMATE ROAD TRIP

This collaborative activity gives your students the chance to work with other students that have similar interests to theirs. It's a great way to build new friendships in your class!

Spotlight on: US regions

Driving question: How can a classmate and I plan a road trip that visits all five regions of the United States?

Audience: Friend

PROCESS

1. Tell your students that they will be planning a road trip with a classmate to visits all five regions of the United States. Print detailed maps of the US for your students and provide them with two or three resources on the different regions of the United States. At least one resource should show a visual of the regions and which states they include. Facilitate as your students use markers or colored pencils to outline each region on their own maps.

2. To properly pair students, give them an interest survey to find out what types of things they like to do. Pair students with similar interests. See the sample interest survey below for a general idea of how to create one for this project.

3. Have students begin with the region that your city or town is in. Have partners work together to research different cities within your region that they may want to visit. Once they agree on a city, have them draw a line on the map from the city or town they live in to the city they're planning to visit. Have them begin an itinerary, writing what they will do in the city they are visiting.

The activities they decide to do will likely match up with what they chose on their interest surveys.

4. Follow the same process with a nearby region. Have students discuss the most efficient order of the regions they will travel to. They should complete the itinerary and map, traveling to one city in each of the five regions.

5. Have each pair present their itinerary, telling about where they are visiting in each region, and what activities they will do there.

INTEREST SURVEY EXAMPLE

Circle the three activities that you're most interested in doing when traveling to a new place. Put a star next to your favorite activity.

- Camping
- Hiking
- Extreme Sports
- Zip-lining
- Swimming
- Shopping
- Taking Pictures
- Eating at Cool Restaurants
- Making New Friends
- Seeing a Play or Other Show

Other Connections: Connect writing to this project by having students use creative writing skills to write a fictional story about their trip to the five regions of the US. Tie in math standards by having students calculate the driving distance in miles. For more advanced grades, they can even calculate the total cost of gas for their road trip.

88 ESTABLISH A COLONY

This project-based learning activity gives students the chance to be creative while exploring persuasive techniques and the 13 colonies. This idea can be used without student devices, but I'm including the steps you would take if your students do have access to devices for video and editing.

Spotlight on: The 13 colonies

Driving question: How can my group create an advertisement to convince the class that our colony was the best of the original 13 colonies?

Audience: Classmates

PROCESS

1. Introduce the 13 English colonies to students with a shared text. Hand each student a blank map of the 13 colonies and have them label the name of each original colony. Make sure they hold on to these maps, because they'll be using them at the end of this project.

2. Tell students that they're going to be assigned a random colony to advertise to the rest of the class. Arrange them into thirteen groups of mixed ability level.

3. Set up a WebQuest or other way to share information on persuasive techniques. My favorite way to do this is to have a digital vocabulary card explaining the persuasive technique and one or two commercials that show the technique.

4. Have each group get ready to research their colony by having them create lists of what they will need to know to advertise that their colony is the best.

5. Give students plenty of time to thoroughly research the history of the colony using the lists they created. Make sure that they focus on the things that made that colony special. While researching, have groups discuss what they learned about their colonies that would appeal to their classmates. For example, the colony of Massachusetts had fish, whales, and forests, so your students can use those details to appeal to the students in the class that like fishing and camping.

6. Have each group create a plan for their advertisement. The advertisement can be a video, poster, pamphlet, or anything else they think will convince the other students in the class that their colony is the best. The more creative the end product, the better!

7. Have students work on creating these advertisements. Students can get feedback from other groups by asking them questions about what they like and dislike. Quick polls are a great way to find out what parts of the advertisement to revise without having the other groups actually see it.

8. As each group presents, have students take quick notes on their colony map page from Step 1. At the end of the presentations, they should have notes on the best aspects of each colony all on this one page.

9. Have students take a vote on which colony they think is the best. Reflect on what persuasive techniques that colony's group used that worked well.

Other Connections: Connect art and multimedia standards to this project by encouraging students to create specific pieces of artwork or videos for their advertisements. You can do this by providing students with a more structured outline of what techniques you expect to see, and which equipment you want them to use.

89 THE MUMMY

In sixth grade, my favorite teacher did a unit where we mummified a chicken. It was totally gross. When my own class began our unit on ancient Egypt, I knew I wanted to avoid the chicken, but I also thought mummification was the perfect starting point for a project-based learning activity.

Spotlight on: Ancient Egypt

Driving question: How can I recreate the mummification process that ancient Egyptians used?

Audience: Open-ended

PROCESS

1. Begin by studying basic life in ancient Egypt. Put together a WebQuest, or provide a variety of articles for students to use to learn more about the topic.

2. Show a video about mummification in ancient Egypt. You can find many free videos on YouTube; just make sure to carefully watch the entire video to ensure that it's appropriate for your class.

3. Ask the question: What can we mummify other than people?

4. Have students further research the process of mummification in ancient Egypt. Come together as a class and share what everyone learned during their research. Make an ordered list of the basic process of mummification.

5. Organize students into pairs. Have them research and discuss what they can mummify. Apples and hot dogs are the easiest, and there are a ton of websites and videos that give step-by-step directions, including the materials they can use as a substitution for what the ancient Egyptians used.

6. Have each pair make a plan for what they want to mummify. Have them write down the steps they will complete for the process and make a list of materials they need.

7. Gather materials. You're going to need a lot of salt, baking soda, and the closest item you can get to linen.

8. After students have received feedback and revised their process, make sure that you individually approve their projects.

9. Have students begin the mummification process. Make sure they have a place to store their mummified item, like a jar.

10. After a week, have students take out their mummified item. Display each item and have students go from item to item with their partner, writing down what they observe of each item.

11. Have students work together as a class to create a video slideshow of all of the items they mummified. Have your high-fliers add subtitles to the video that tell about the process of mummification and what they learned during the project. My software of choice for this is iMovie, but there are many options.

12. For their end product, have them choose their audience. Who do they think would benefit from learning how to mummify something?

Other Connections: Tie in science standards by learning about how salt and baking soda remove the water from a mummified item, making it hard for bacteria to survive and cause decay.

90 DOCUMENTING IMMIGRATION

Using video is a great way for students to learn a different way to tell a story. In this project, students will use devices or video cameras to create an immigration documentary as a class.

Spotlight on: Immigration

Driving question: How can we create a documentary that teaches kids our age about the history of immigration?

Audience: Other students

PROCESS

1. Before beginning, figure out what tools you have available to complete this project. What devices can your students use to record and edit video and audio? What software or apps will they use?

2. Tell students that they will be working on a project as a class. Introduce the topic by defining immigration and leading a discussion. Ask students if they have any friends or family members that recently emigrated from another country.

3. Have students work in pairs to research the history of immigration. Tie in standards that relate to the history of immigration, such as Ellis Island. Have students collect details, including images, that they can use to portray the history of immigration at the beginning of the documentary.

4. Make a list of things that need to be done for the documentary. Focus on content needed and the order the content will appear in the film.

5. Split students into groups with specific tasks from your list. For example, have one group create an introduction that defines immigration, while another creates a video timeline that shows the events that will be covered in the documentary. Have other groups focus on specific events, or finding images and video to add to the documentary.

6. Bring in friends or family members of the students that have experience with immigration, either themselves or from hearing stories from an older relative. Have students interview these people for the documentary. Record them, if possible.

7. Once each piece of the film is fully edited and ready to go, put all pieces of the film together. Work as a class to add any final touches (e.g., music), and publish the film.

8. Watch the completed film as a class. Share it with everyone that participated. Upload the video online to share with other kids interested in immigration.

Other Connections: If you're using this project with fifth graders or older students, you can incorporate opinion writing by reading articles about current immigration issues and forming opinions to write an essay. This is a very relevant topic, especially if you live in a border town.

91 NATIVE AMERICAN ART EXHIBIT

This activity is open-ended so that you can use it for any specific tribes or regions. Adjust the driving question to reflect the tribes or region that you'll be inquiring about during this project.

Spotlight on: Native American cultures

Driving question: How can we recreate something beautiful and functional from a Native American culture for an art exhibit?

Audience: People of all ages

PROCESS

1. Before beginning, determine where and when your art exhibit will be displayed. It can be displayed somewhere in your school, but I suggest trying to make a connection in the community to give this art exhibit a home where it will be seen by more people. A local art gallery, kids museum, or government building would be a great choice. You'd be surprised how many people are happy to connect with a classroom to display something unique at their location.

2. Discuss the project parameters with your students. Tell them that they will be working together to research the Native American culture, while individually looking for ideas of something beautiful and functional that they can recreate for the class art exhibit.

3. Introduce the topic by reading a picture book or short passage to your students about the Native American culture they will be studying. Have them create a list of questions about the culture.

4. As a class, make a list of the different aspects of the culture that students should learn about. These can be aspects of life like dress, family structure, and traditions.

5. Have students work in pairs or small groups to research their questions and any aspects of Native American life from their lists. As students conduct their research, remind them to look for something beautiful and functional they would like to recreate for the art exhibit. Tell them that they are looking for something to build or design, and not just something to draw on flat paper.

6. Have each individual student decide what item from the Native American culture they want to recreate for the exhibit. Have students further research their items, sketch their ideas on paper, revise, and then create.

7. Discuss how students can explain the significance of the items. They will need to come up with an idea that is appropriate for all ages. This could be something like a verbal recording that goes behind the item, or a sign with pictures and text to hang next to it.

8. Set up the exhibit. If the exhibit is off site, send home information to parents on how to view the exhibit with their student. Take lots of photos after the exhibit is set up.

9. If time allows, have each student share a little about what they created, and what it represents in the Native American culture.

Other Connections: Integrate STEM into this project by adjusting it so that students are building a structure for the art exhibit. If you search online for "Native American structures," you'll see that there are several types of structures that your students could build.

92 CLASSROOM GOVERNMENT

This is a year-long project that will take a couple of weeks to establish, but that you'll use any time a decision needs to be made for the classroom. Not only does this give students more decisions to make in class, but it continually reminds them of the roles and purpose of the three branches of government.

Spotlight on: Branches of government

Driving question: How can we form a classroom government using the three branches of government that the United States uses?

Audience: Classmates

PROCESS

1. Choose something that you need your students to decide on before beginning the project. This could be something like a field trip location, the next class read aloud, or which service project to do.

2. Tell students that all class decisions will now be made using the same setup as the United States Government. Let them know that they will have to learn more about the three branches of government in order to assign roles to different people in the class.

3. Have students work in pairs to learn more about the three branches of government. Then, have several pairs get together in larger groups to discuss what they learned and why the government is set up this way. Ask students how this system would help your class make decisions without one person taking charge of everything.

4. Ask students which branch they're most interested in. Make a list of all of the students who are most interested in each branch.

5. Have students return to the research to find out how positions in the executive branch are filled. Have all students vote to choose a president, choosing from the list of people interested in the executive branch. Have the president choose a vice president to help them make decisions.

6. Make a list of the students most interested in the judicial branch. Research how many justices there are and how they are chosen. Have the president and vice president select nine justices from the list of interested students. You can reduce this number to make sure the house and senate are balanced, depending on your class size.

7. Have the students research the legislative branch. This is a bit more complex, but to simplify it, place all of the remaining students in this branch. Split these students into the house (75 percent of students) and the senate (25 percent of students).

8. Have your three branches work together to make the class decision selected in Step 1. Have the legislative branch debate the different choices. You can elaborate on how a bill becomes a law using this step, or keep it simple by having a majority vote. Next, send the decision to the president and vice president. They can agree or disagree. Lastly, have the judicial branch check the decision to make sure it's an appropriate decision for the good of the class.

9. Have students write a reflection on the process. Have them make class decisions using the same process for the rest of the year. Have them journal about it each time.

Other Connections: This project goes very well with the Create a Bill project (page 195). Merging the two would allow your students to do more in-depth research and discussion on the topics included.

93 STORIES FROM SEPTEMBER 11

Recording oral histories is a great way to preserve memories that individuals have about historical events. This would be a great project for you and your class to complete in the weeks leading up to September 11.

Spotlight on: 9/11 terrorist attacks

Driving question: How can we record and share oral histories about the 9/11 terrorist attacks?

Audience: People who want to know more about September 11

PROCESS

1. Determine what equipment you have available for recording oral histories. It can be as simple as using the built-in microphone on a cell phone or tablet. I like to keep a couple cheap noise reduction microphones in my classroom for students to use on projects like this.

2. Introduce the topic to your students by reading about the tragic events. Have your students discuss 9/11 with their families, asking their parents and grandparents if they have stories about how they experienced 9/11. Even a story about watching the news reports while it happened would be great for an oral history.

3. As a class, plan for how you will record these oral histories. Do your students have the capability to each record someone at home tell their story about 9/11? If they take home devices, then this is a fairly easy task. If not, bring in parent or staff volunteers so that students can record at school with your equipment.

4. Discuss interview questions, length of interviews, and the types of stories students should look for to bring the history alive.

5. Have your students start to think about how they can publicly share the oral histories. Do they want to upload them to a website to share? Merge them all together and upload to YouTube? Discuss and make a tentative decision on how they will be shared.

6. Have students conduct the interviews. Record everything. After the recording is finished, students can edit out mistakes and details that aren't important.

7. Listen to pieces of the recordings as a class. Take notes on each and give feedback. This is a great way to critique while also learning more about 9/11 from the oral histories.

8. Finalize the recordings. Make the final decision on how the class will publish these.

9. Publish the finished oral history recordings and share with everyone that participated.

Other Connections: Bring in someone from a local historical society to talk about how oral histories are used. Find and listen to oral histories from other historical events.

94 LIVING HISTORY: THE PRESIDENTS

This project provides your students with a more in-depth look at the presidents and the different time periods they served in. A living history can be done with any group of historical figures, but the presidents are my all-time favorite group to use it with.

Spotlight on: US presidents

Driving question: How can we bring a president to life in order to educate students about them?

Audience: Other students in your school

PROCESS

1. Begin by having students inquire about some of the presidents. This can be done using a WebQuest, books, or a combination of both. Students should have access to information about each president, but have them each choose and read about just a few. Students will be drawn to different presidents.

2. Divide students into groups of two or three. Have each group choose a president that they think made a big difference in the history of our country. Students should continue their inquiry into different presidents until they land on one that they think made a significant difference.

3. Once each group selects a president, come together as a class to plan for how students will continue their research. Have students come up with an organizer to record information, as well as a list of questions they should answer about the presidents.

4. Have students complete their research. Stop to discuss, provide feedback, and ask new questions about the presidents.

5. As a class, discuss how to display the presidents in the exhibit. This is a living history, so the students need to show the president alive in some way. This can be done in many ways, such as dressing up as the presidents, or setting up audio recordings of speeches the presidents gave.

6. Put on the living history exhibit. Invite other classes that are studying the presidents to come view the exhibit.

7. To make the exhibit meaningful, have students put together an activity that the visiting students have to do. It can be something simple, like having them vote for the president they think made the biggest difference in history. Or it can be more complex, like having a timeline they fill in with information about each president in the exhibit.

Other Connections: Incorporate informational writing into this project by having students write essays about their chosen president.

95 STATE QUILT FUNDRAISER

I always try to connect our fundraisers with valuable learning opportunities. This is another project that does this, incorporating social studies, sewing, and presentation skills.

Spotlight on: State history

Driving question: How can we create a quilt that portrays the beautiful history of our state that someone from the community will want to buy to display in their home or business?

Audience: Parents and community members

PROCESS

1. Before beginning, send home a letter telling parents about this project and asking for volunteers. You will need supplies donated and adult help for the sewing portion. I highly suggest finding a family member or someone in the community that is an experienced quilter to help guide students and sew the entire quilt together. Many quilting clubs do outreach and fundraising, so reach out to your local club, if you have one.

2. Introduce the project by giving your students a basic sewing lesson. Teach them how to thread a needle and sew two scraps together.

3. Set up a structure for your students to inquire about your local state history. Make a "Need to Know" list using your standards. As a class, create a timeline they can fill in as they learn about the important events in your state's history. Complete research independently or in small groups.

4. After students have had plenty of time to learn about the state's history, come together as a class to create a formal timeline. Get student input on how to take the events from the timeline and represent them on the quilt. Discuss other items that should be on the quilt, such as the state flag, bird, and motto.

5. Have each student pick what they want to create from your timeline and list. Write their names next to the item or event they're representing.

6. Have a quilter come in and talk to students about how they will create their squares for the quilt. Help students create a step-by-step list of what they need to do, from designing the quilt to sewing the squares.

7. Allow students to work in small groups as they design their individual squares. Encourage them to get feedback from their groups as they design, and to do additional research on the items or events they're representing in their quilt square. Discuss why it's important to pay attention to detail when representing history on their quilt square.

8. Make a list of the necessary supplies to create the quilt squares. The colors of cloth and thread you'll need depend on each student's design.

9. Finalize designs. Bring in parent or community volunteers to help students with cutting and sewing their quilt squares.

10. Have a quilter put together the big quilt. In the meantime, have students create a plan for how they will advertise the quilt auction. Discuss the type of people that would spend money on this quilt. Parents will want it because it was created by their class, but what about business owners that want to display it at their business? What about local historical societies? Brainstorm how to advertise this fundraiser to those people, as well as to parents. The goal is to raise as much money as possible, and for that, you will need a large group of people interested in the quilt.

11. Once the quilt is finished, have students take pictures of it and prepare for the auction. Then, auction off the quilt.

Other Connections: This project already has some amazing skills built in, in addition to learning about your state's history. You can add in a math component by having students determine what the school or class should purchase with the money raised.

96 OUR IDEAL COMMUNITY

A lot of my projects revolve around reaching out to the local community. In this project-based learning activity, students learn about how a community runs.

Spotlight on: Local community and government

Driving question: How can we create an ideal community plan that helps our local government get ideas for improving our community?

Audience: Local government or city council

PROCESS

1. Make a connection with people in the local government before beginning. The first place I would start is the city council. This is a fairly large group of people, so you will probably be able to convince at least two or three to participate in this project. You will also need to find people available to talk about the different city services, like parks and recreation, water and trash, etc.

2. Begin by brainstorming the parts of your community. Your initial list may include schools, businesses, police and fire stations, and the local government.

3. Tell students that they will be learning about all of the aspects of your local community in order to make a plan for an ideal community. These plans will be submitted to the city council to give them ideas to make the community better.

4. Gather and share reading materials for students to read and discuss the different aspects of the community. I usually gather pamphlets from the city, maps of important areas (a main street or downtown area, if you have one), and historical photos of what the city looked like in the past. Have students read about these community pieces, and work together to extend your list of the parts of our community. This is a great time to bring in speakers to talk about city services, local businesses, and the local government.

5. Help students start a journal of things they see in the community that they think need to be improved. Encourage them to take this journal home and add to it any time they leave the house. They can write down issues they experience while out with their families, like broken equipment in a local park, difficulty parking in downtown, or a lack of a certain store or service. Tell students to ask other people how they think the community can be improved, and to write down what those people say.

6. Have each student pinpoint an aspect of the community that they want to improve. Group students that choose similar aspects. For example, if there are three students that noticed that a park nearby has a lot of broken equipment, group them together to work on that issue. Another group might work on a plan to bring a better selection of restaurants to the city.

7. Facilitate while each group discusses and researches how to improve their piece of the community. Have them come up with a way to present their ideas to the city council. For example, the group with broken equipment can create a park design that shows new equipment. The group working on bringing new restaurants to the city can create a map of the best locations for these restaurants and craft a letter telling businesses why they should build their next restaurant in this city.

8. After individual projects have been completed, come together as a class to plan how you will present all of these different things to the city council.

9. Present all of the student ideas to the city council. You can attend an actual meeting, or ask some of the city council members to visit you at your school.

Other Connections: Work together to create a class book called "Our Ideal Community." Have each student write a descriptive piece on one thing they want to improve in the community, and include an illustration. Share copies of the book with the city council.

97 VIRTUAL MUSEUM

This is a project-based learning activity that requires the use of technology. It makes connections to other students around the world, so if you do have access to student devices, it's a great project to try! It can easily be modified for almost any social studies topic you want.

Spotlight on: The American Revolution

Driving question: How can we create a virtual museum in order to give people easy access to free, visual information on the American Revolution?

Audience: Students around the world studying the American Revolution

PROCESS

1. Begin by providing students with links to virtual tours from a few different museums. Have students make a list of the content they found in the virtual tours.

2. Discuss the idea of a completely digital museum. What would the benefits be? Who would view this content?

3. Make a list of the American Revolution concepts you have been or will be learning about. I prefer to organize students into groups based on the topics they're most interested, and then use the completed museum and additional activities to help them learn about the parts that they didn't inquire about.

4. Spend a good deal of time having groups do in-depth inquiry into the topic they chose. Provide them with several examples of virtual museum exhibits. Have students discuss ideas for their topic's exhibit as they do their initial research.

5. Have groups begin sketching ideas for their exhibits. Have them decide what they will build for their exhibit and what information needs to be included to explain the specific American Revolution topic.

6. Have students begin building exhibits. Continue doing inquiry, discussion, and critique.

7. Finalize each individual exhibit display. Have students place their exhibits in front of a "green screen" (a large green cloth or paper works). Film using a green screen video app on student devices (www.instructables.com/id/How-to-make-a-Green-Screen-video-from-an-App). Have students find background images online that can replace the green screen to make it look more like a real museum. Images like a brick wall or indoor backgrounds would work well.

8. Save all videos to one folder in Google Drive. Show groups how to create QR codes using the link to their video in Google Drive.

9. Discuss the digital layout of the museum. Which topics should have their exhibits close to each other on the museum layout?

10. As a class, use a drawing app to create the museum's digital layout using a drawing app like Pixie. Julie Smith shared a great digital zoo layout on her blog that might help you get an idea of what a digital layout design looks like (www.thetechieteacher .net/2015/03/wonderful-wacky-zoo-project.html).

11. Share the links to each video. If you print the layout to share, you can print the QR codes to place on the corresponding area of the layout. Students can scan these codes with their devices and instantly see the videos. To share digitally, you can save the museum layout as an image and upload it to an image map generator (imagemap-generator.dariodomi.de). Image map generators allow you to add different links to each area of an image, so that when people click on an area of the museum layout, it will automatically take them to associated video using the Google Drive share link! You can then add the image map to your class website, or a website you make for the digital museum.

12. Have students test out their digital museum to make sure it's easy to access the information. Have them come up with ideas on how to share this awesome resource with people interested in the American Revolution.

Other Connections: If you find that your students are really interested in graphic design and website building, spend time putting together a complete website for the virtual museum. You can take it as far as your class wants to!

98 RESOURCES FOR STUDENTS WITH DISABILITIES

This is another project that can easily be modified for any social studies topic. It connects with an important part of your school and community: students with disabilities.

Spotlight on: Landforms (geography)

Driving question: How can we create learning resources for students in the community with disabilities?

Audience: Students with disabilities

PROCESS

1. Before beginning, fill your classroom with books on different disabilities. I'm usually able to find 10 to 15 just at my local library.

2. If you can, partner with a group in your community that works with kids with disabilities. You can focus on one disability in particular for this project, or make a list of multiple disabilities that kids in your school and community have. For this example, the class will focus on multiple disabilities.

3. Tell your students that you will be learning about landforms in class, and that their goal is to make the information they're learning about accessible for students with disabilities.

4. Divide students into groups and assign each group a disability to make modified lessons for. Each group will be creating learning materials on mountains, valleys, plateaus, glaciers, hills, loesses, and plains.

5. Bring in experts to discuss the disabilities that your groups are focusing on. This can be someone from a group in your community, a parent of a child with the disability, or an adult with the disability. Have students prepare questions to ask the speaker about the types of materials that would help kids with this disability learn about landforms.

6. Facilitate while each group completes research into landforms. Have them use a variety of reading materials, images, and videos to learn more about the landforms.

7. Discuss how students can modify these materials to make them accessible for students with disabilities.

8. Have each group create a five- to ten-minute lesson on landforms, with materials that support their assigned disability.

- Presentation option 1: Have students do the lesson with a student that has this disability.

- Presentation option 2: Have students make a video to upload to YouTube giving their lesson and explaining how it's modified for the disability. This would be a great resource for teachers and parents that want to help a student with this disability learn about this landform.

Other Connections: Use the eagerness your students have during this project to complete a service project where you raise money for a group that supports people with disabilities.

99 DOES HISTORY REPEAT ITSELF?

The Mayan culture is a fun topic to study, but students often miss some of the important lessons they can learn from the Mayans. This project merges the Mayan culture with our present-day culture in a very engaging way!

Spotlight on: Mayan civilization

Driving question: How can we create an action plan to solve a problem that both the Mayans and present-day people share?

Audience: Community

PROCESS

1. Introduce the basic facts about the Mayans. Show students photos relating to different aspects of the Mayan culture. Have students write questions they have about the Mayans.

2. Inquire into student questions. Create an organizer for taking notes about the different aspects of Mayan culture.

3. Answer the question: What do researchers think caused the Mayan civilization to collapse? Make a list of some of the things researchers think led to the collapse.

4. Discuss similarities to present-day issues. Make a class list of connected issues, including overpopulation, military conflict, and drought (link this to climate change). Ask: Does history repeat itself?

5. Have students briefly discuss possible solutions to each issue. Help students choose the issue they're most interested in, then group them based on this choice.

6. Move the focus from Mayan civilization to present-day issues. After extensive group discussion, have students begin to write their action plan. The action plan should have five parts:

- Identify goals for the solution.

- Create tasks to meet these goals.

- Assign tasks to the people that can best perform them (this is not necessarily students—it could be government officials and community leaders).

- Prioritize the tasks. A flowchart is a great way to accomplish this.

- Choose dates to meet goals and to evaluate the effectiveness of the action plan.

7. After students have had plenty of time to write their action plan, get feedback, and revise, have them brainstorm ideas for how they will present this action plan to the people that need to be involved. The type of presentation they create should be customized to their individual audience. For example, if the people they need involved are the president of the United States, Congress, and the EPA, then it would probably be best to present the information in written form through a letter or email. If the people involved are kids (the next generation), then something like a graphic novel might be a good way to present the plan.

8. Facilitate while each group finalizes their presentation of the action plan.

9. Send the action plans to the people and groups involved. You will get great feedback from most people that receive it!

Other Connections: Connect persuasive writing to this project by teaching students techniques that they can include in a preface to their action plans.

100 BREAKING NEWS

In the ELA section of this book, the Young Journalists project offers some ideas for a school newspaper. This project is similar, except the focus goes beyond the school and community's events. In this activity, students spend time every week reading about the current events in the world and choosing the ones they want to share about with other students.

Spotlight on: Current events

Driving question: How can I share weekly news with kids my age to keep them informed about important news?

Audience: Students and families

PROCESS

1. Set aside a time each week, or every other week, to read about current events. Before beginning, determine how your students will learn about current events. For the older students (fifth grade and up), I love CNN's Student News (www.edition.cnn.com/studentnews). Newsela is a great site for all ages. Scholastic also has a fantastic magazine for current events if your school is willing to order those.

2. Discuss with your students how they want to publish this weekly news. Let them decide if they want to do it in print, digitally (written), or as an online weekly news video.

3. Begin your first week by providing your students with a short list of news stories on current events. Allow students time to read and discuss the stories.

4. Group students based on which story they're most interested in. Not every story needs to be represented.

5. Work together to organize the weekly news. Make a list of everything the class wants to include. If they chose to publish a traditional newspaper, look at some of the articles in a newspaper to help make a list of what to include. If they chose to do a video show, make a list of segments and any props or technology needed.

6. Have each group work on a piece of the newspaper or news show in relation to the current event they chose.

7. Publish the first "issue" in print or online.

8. Continue this weekly or biweekly, including new current events.

Other Connections: I don't suggest doing this and the school newspaper listed in the ELA section at the same time, but you can easily incorporate informational writing skills into this project. If students choose to do a news show, have them script it out. Discuss the importance of editing when doing a scripted news show. It might be funny to the audience when a newscaster reads something wrong, but it's embarrassing for the student!

CHAPTER 7

PROJECT WRAP-UP

Many teachers I work with tell me that they struggle with ending their project-based learning. Although the end point is different from project to project, I do have some tips for an effective wrap-up.

ENDING THE PROJECT

1. Set an End Date

In Chapter 2, I showed you how to create a pacing calendar when planning your PBL. It's essential to have an end date in mind. As your students finish up the research portion of their projects, start to set more exact deadlines for end products and presentations. Add deadlines to your class calendar, and have students add them to their own calendars. Remind students of deadlines each day, and help them set up small daily goals to help them manage their time.

2. Plan Your Wrap-Up Day

If you get to the last day of the project and students simply turn in their projects, it's going to be very underwhelming for everyone. The last day of your project should include important activities, like presenting to your audience and reflecting on the project.

Not every wrap-up day needs to include a formal presentation. It's important to mix things up when you're doing project-based learning throughout the year. You'll notice that the included project ideas conclude in many different ways. Some end by mailing letters, while others end with an event or fundraiser. No matter what you plan for your wrap-up day, it should be both fun and meaningful.

3. Use Your Audience

Deadlines are much more motivating when there are real people waiting to see what you've done. Remind your students that their audience is waiting for their products. Spend some time discussing how their products will help a group of people.

4. Keep the Momentum Going

Your students shouldn't lose interest in the topic just because it's the last day of the project. Use the wrap-up day as a stepping-stone into a new project, or to extend the learning using one of the connections listed in each project under "Other Connections."

FORMAL PRESENTATIONS

If a formal presentation is an appropriate way to end the project you're working on, I have a couple recommendations to make this a meaningful experience for your students.

First of all, make sure that end products are presented to the target audience. Presenting to people in the school is only appropriate if that is an authentic audience for that project. Any projects around school improvement or helping students learn something new can use an audience of students and staff at the school. If the audience is their own family members, then it's reasonable for them to present their end products to their family at home.

No matter who your audience is, don't have presentation blocks that are longer than 20 minutes, unless their presentations are very interactive. If you've ever done back-to-back presentations where students come up in groups and share posters on the same topic, you understand the struggle this creates for the audience. The best way to have students present to an audience is to allow them to interact with their audience in small groups. Think about the way science fairs are run. They don't have each student stand in front of everyone and present. Instead, students present to small groups of people as they come up to view their projects. This engages the audience much more, while allowing for students to get instant feedback.

ASSESSMENT

Rubrics are the most common way to grade project-based learning. I use a combination of three items for assessment:

1. Rubrics

2. Self-Assessment

3. Reflection

USING RUBRICS

It's important to create a rubric to use for the project before your students begin. The rubric should cover every aspect of the process of the project, not just the end product. It should also be open-ended, to allow for a variety of processes and products. You can often modify skill rubrics to fit the project. For example, our state provides a rubric for informational writing that we're required to use. When creating my rubrics for projects that include informational writing, I copy and paste the components from that rubric into my project rubric. The other sections of the rubric cover the 21st-century skills I want students to focus on for that particular project, such as collaboration and innovation. I also add in any requirements I have given for the final product.

The following is an example of a simple rubric for the animal habitats project idea in Chapter 2.

SAMPLE RUBRIC: ANIMAL HABITATS

	4	3	2	1
RESEARCH AND INFORMATION GATHERING	Thorough research was done for their habitat. Detailed note pages are filled with accurate information on the topic. Sources are listed.	Satisfactory research was done for their habitat. One or two note pages have accurate information on the topic. Sources are listed.	Little research has been done. Less than a page of notes has accurate information on the topic. Sources may not be included.	Very little effort was put into research.

	4	3	2	1
PLANNING AND CRITICAL THINKING	The student made decisions for their habitat that make sense. They can support all of their decisions with details from the text.	The student made decisions for their habitat that make sense. They can support some of their decisions with details from the text.	Some decisions for their habitat do not make sense. The student struggles to explain why they made these choices.	Planning is missing and decisions were not made.
END PRODUCT: WRITTEN PLAN	Written plan has complete sentences and no grammatical and spelling errors.	Written plan has complete sentences and some grammatical and spelling errors.	Written plan does not have complete sentences and has several grammatical and spelling errors.	Written plan is not complete, or is illegible.
END PRODUCT: HABITAT DESIGN	Habitat design is appropriate for the chosen animal. The design includes innovative elements.	No innovative elements are included in the design, but the habitat is appropriate for the chosen animal.	Habitat design is complete, but some essential elements are missing.	Habitat design is incomplete.
END PRODUCT: HABITAT PRESENTATION	Student is well prepared to present their information to their audience. Their presentation answers the driving question in a dynamic, easy-to-understand format.	Student is somewhat prepared to present their information to their audience. Their presentation answers the driving question in an easy-to-understand format.	Student is unprepared to present their information to their audience. Their presentation somewhat answers the driving question, but the focus is unclear.	Student is unprepared to present their information to their audience. Their presentation does not address the driving question.

253

Make sure to slightly alter your original rubric to create a student-friendly rubric for your students to use. This is essential in guiding students toward their goals, and will be used when students complete their self-assessments.

SELF-ASSESSMENT AND REFLECTION

Students are surprisingly honest when you ask them to self-assess. Most will tell you exactly how much effort they did, or did not, put into a project. Self-assessment should be factored into their project grades for one key reason: Some students do not have the skill level of your high-achievers, but they put in way more effort. This effort should be rewarded when grading. You will likely notice this effort when you are facilitating a project, but self-assessment helps you really pinpoint the effort level of each student.

If one of your concerns about PBL is that some students will be doing more work in the group than others, I encourage you to also incorporate multiple opportunities for self-assessment during the project.

Reflection is another key piece of assessment. I encourage you, as the teacher, to reflect on each part of the project. You can use your own reflection as a model to help your students learn how to reflect on their work.

Self-assessment and reflection can be assigned in a few ways:

1. Have students journal daily about their progress on the project.

2. Give students the rubric and have them circle the rating they would give their work. Have them add a written explanation.

3. Verbally ask students questions about the quality of their work and record the answers.

4. Guide students to write a reflection paragraph or essay at the end of the project.

FINAL THOUGHTS

Teaching is one of the most difficult professions to be in. It's a constant balancing act between state standards, required assessments, and curriculum calendars. You may not be able to implement project-based learning in the way that this book suggests, and that's OK. What I really want to see as the result of this book is your being able to share your passions with your students. Choose a project topic that calls to you. Implement the project in a way that works for you and your classroom. Incorporate any suggestions that work for you, and ignore the ones that don't.

The fact that you've purchased and read this book means that you truly care about your students and their learning. Thank you for all that you do for your students!

APPENDIX

COMMON ISSUES

Just like with anything in teaching, there are going to be problems to work out when you implement project-based learning. Below are some of the common issues I've heard from teachers using PBL in their classes. As you begin your projects, keep the suggestions below in mind when you encounter these problems. If you encounter an issue that's not on this list, immediately seek out help from other teachers (online or in your building) that do project-based learning. If you're having an issue, chances are that other teachers have had the issue, as well.

I'm struggling with time management. My students have been researching for days and never seem to get anywhere.

This was one of my biggest problems when our students first got their hands on their own technology. We were two days into presentation prep during my first PBL activity that implemented technology and some students were still scrolling through Google for the perfect images. I quickly realized that you need goals and structure for each section of your project. Without some sort of structure, your students can easily fall down the rabbit hole of searching through websites, images, and videos. My solution was to make a folder of 20 images for my students to use in their presentations. Another good way to keep research focused is to have your students help you create an organizer to use to collect the information they need. Have them check off each section as they get the information. If they're still researching for hours, I suggest giving them a short list of resources they can use to complete their research; this will cut down the time they spend researching. The most important thing to do when having time-management problems is to plan and structure smaller blocks within the project. Sit down with your students and create a timeline with deadlines for each part of the project.

My students aren't self-starters and need a lot of direction.

This is absolutely the case in most classrooms. We don't give students the chance to be independent from us enough for them to have these skills—yet. One thing you can do to help is have your students work with you to create task lists for each day. Stop and discuss how far students have progressed on their lists, and encourage them to add tasks. Create a running question list that students can add to as they ask and answer questions. If a student or group is stuck, they can view the question list to get ideas of what others are inquiring about. You will have to do a lot of modeling of how you want students to act during project-based learning, but it will get easier.

I have a huge class, and I'm having trouble keeping everyone on track.

Accountability is key in PBL. If you give 35 students too much freedom, you will have chaos. My suggestion for when you have trouble keeping students on track during a project is to cut it into smaller segments. Track how long it takes your students to drift away from their tasks, then plan to change gears or include some sort of discussion or critique when you reach this time marker. So if your students get off task after about 45 minutes, then change gears every 40 minutes. It's all about building a structure where students have a voice and a choice, but also stay focused and on track.

I have a student in my classroom with special needs.

This is a great thing! There's nothing more rewarding than finding a way for students with special needs to be more involved in your class. The flexibility of project-based learning allows for everyone to be included. When you initially plan your project, focus on how you will accommodate this student. It may be as easy as placing them with a partner that already helps them out in the classroom. You can provide alternative materials for the research portions, and provide additional support in the areas they need it.

My students are very low performing academically. I worry that they will struggle with project-based learning because of this.

Project-based learning is very effective with students that struggle with traditional instruction. You'd be surprised how well they respond when presented with a fun and engaging project instead of the teach–practice–assess model. When you're planning the content that your students will be working with, prepare materials that are easily accessible at their current level. I'm a strong believer in starting at the student's level and building them up from there. If I have a group of fifth-grade students that read at a first-grade level, I'm not going to give them a fifth-grade reading passage and then scratch my head about why they're struggling. I'm going to give them access to text at the first- and second-grade levels, with extra small group support and discussion.

I have a handful of high-achieving students that finish things quickly.

Don't assign these students to groups or partners that really struggle. This creates a situation where the struggling student doesn't put as much effort in, and the high-achieving student ends up working at a lower level. You want to group these students together, or with other students that are almost in the high-achiever category. These students should have more freedom to go above and beyond during the project. They should be creating tasks that are more challenging for themselves and using more advanced technology, if you have access to it.

I'm required to put a weekly grade in the gradebook, but I only seem to have one final grade during my PBL activities.

Even if you don't have grading requirements, it's important that students know how they're doing throughout the project. One final grade or feedback opportunity just doesn't cut it. If you build in critique and revision, students will be constantly getting feedback. You can assign a grade based on their effort during the revision process. You can also ask them questions about the skills they're using and give them a skill grade. Most importantly, I always use a rubric that covers several aspects of the project, not just the end product.

RESOURCES

STEM

Water Habitats by Molly Aloian and Bobbie Kalman

The Drop in My Drink: The Story of Water on Our Planet by Meredith Hooper

climate.nasa.gov Up-to-date climate change news and data

climatekids.nasa.gov Climate change information with activities, games, and video for kids

spc.noaa.gov National Weather Service's Storm Prediction Center

az.pbslearningmedia.org/resource/nat15.sci.lisci.anihome/habitat-animal-homes Animal habitats resource

https://earthquake.usgs.gov/earthquakes/map Recent earthquake map *www.swfwmd.state.fl.us/conservation/thepowerof10* Water use calculator

HISTORY AND CURRENT EVENTS

Who Was Martin Luther King, Jr.? by Bonnie Bader

Roughing It on the Oregon Trail by Diane Stanley

The Flag We Love by Pam Muñoz Ryan

www.newsela.com News articles written for different reading levels

www.edition.cnn.com/studentnews Daily news stories for kids fifth grade and up

sn3.scholastic.com Current events and news aligned to grade level

MEMOIRS

El Deafo by Cece Bell

Ashley Bryan: Words to My Life's Song by Ashley Bryan

Bigmama's by Donald Crews

Ugly by Robert Hoge

Saturdays and Teacakes by Lester Laminack

My Rotten Redheaded Older Brother by Patricia Polacco

TEAMWORK

Swimmy by Leo Lionni

Up the Creek by Nicholas Oldland

The Junkyard Wonders by Patricia Polacco

How the Crayons Saved the Rainbow by Monica Sweeney

PERSERVERENCE

The Noisy Paint Box by Barb Rosenstock

The Most Magnificant Thing by Ashley Spires

Emmanuel's Dream by Laurie Ann Thompson

A Chair for My Mother by Vera B. Williams

ENTREPRENEURSHIP

Whoosh!: Lonnie Johnson's Super-Soaking Stream of Inventions by Chris Barton

Be a Young Entrepreneur by Adam Sutherland

Better Than a Lemonade Stand!: Small Business Ideas for Kids by Daryl Bernstein

Kidpreneurs: Young Entrepreneurs with Big Ideas! by Adam Toren

If I Built a Car by Chris Van Dusen

www.bizkids.com Offers videos about entrepreneurship

www.theparkcatalog.com Park equipment catalog

www.youtube.com/user/MoneySmartKid Financial literacy videos for kids

WEB/TECHNOLOGY RESOURCES

www.sweetsearch.com Safe search engine for students

imagemap-generator.dariodomi.de Makes an image with clickable pieces to send your students to different web resources

www.instructables.com/id/How-to-make-a-Green-Screen-video-from-an-App Instructional video on how to make a green screen

www.thetechieteacher.net/2015/03/wonderful-wacky-zoo-project .html Interactive zoo map example (possible student output)

www.zinepal.com Enables you to create ebooks from online content

ACKNOWLEDGMENTS

First and foremost, the content of this book comes from the experiences I've had with my amazing students. I have to thank them for all that they've taught me during project-based learning. Their hard work and continual feedback has helped me refine my teaching in many ways.

The collaboration I've had with other teachers has been indispensable. Without the teachers I've worked with, in person and online, I would not have even known where to start with this book. I'd like to say thank you to all the teachers that have shared their project-based learning experiences and struggles with me.

This book would not have been possible without the support of my family and friends. To my husband Peter, thank you for encouraging me to follow my passions, and for making countless sacrifices to support me. Thank you to all of the friends and family that have cheered me on during the writing of this book.

ABOUT THE AUTHOR

APRIL SMITH is a teacher, blogger, and lover of all hands-on teaching methods. She began using project-based learning in her fifth-grade classroom in 2011. As she learned more about the methods, she began merging activity ideas and the different parts of PBL to bring authentic learning experiences to her students. She began integrating standards and creating structures that allow students to have voice and choice while maintaining order. April was recognized as Intermediate Teacher of the Year for the county in 2015. She now works remotely with K–5 teachers and districts that are looking to replace traditional teaching methods with project-based learning.